# America can live *Happily* Ever After

*Creating Good Citizens*

Elizabeth Wiley MA JD, Pomo Elder

Order this book online at www.trafford.com
or email orders@trafford.com

Most Trafford titles are also available at major online book retailers.

Print information available on the last page.

ISBN: 978-1-4907-9241-5 (sc)
ISBN: 978-1-4907-9242-2 (e)

*Trafford rev.  11/30/2018*

 www.trafford.com
North America & international
toll-free: 1 888 232 4444 (USA & Canada)
fax: 812 355 4082

# INTRODUCTION

This book is a challenge, a hope, a push to make yourself, your family and your city, county, state and our nation, along with the world a better place for everyone, and everything It is a challenge to YOU to find what you personally NEED and want to "live happily ever after…" and to create the changes needed to make that a reality. It is a challenge to you to find out what your family, job, block, or apartment floor need to "live happily ever after…" and to create the changes needed to make that a reality.

WARNING: this book is written by retired old persons, with concussions and brain injuries thanks to those who injure others without concern. This is NOT an APA book written for grammar critics. Do not bother to write and criticize, we do NOT read or consider mean people's thoughts on our use of commas, semi colons, or colons or language use. Go bother the mean people, the criminals, drunk drivers, the corporate leaders and lawyers, and politicians who allow horrible injury to others without care, or consequence.

Abraham Lincoln is alleged to have said, "YOU will be as happy as you make up your mind to be". It is a key to the gateway of being happy. Eleanor Roosevelt is alleged to have said it is up to each of us to choose to let the opinions and criticism of others harm us, or NOT. Joyce Meyer invented the excuse bag, and the God bag. She took real handbags, and in one put the excuses to not live happily ever after, and in the other put those excuses, one by one, handing them over to God as each person used those burdens as building blocks, or stepping stones, rather than roadblocks, to let them find a way to help themselves and others avoid the pitfalls, and/or to overcome the injury and inner pain of real life injuries.

Most of our work is done with veterans, first responders, and high risk youth and their families. Most of them, if not all, have excuse bags overflowing, yet most of them learn to admit, address and give their excuses to the God bag. In some retreats for women veterans, and single parent mothers sent to us in mandatory Court ordered programs to earm custody of their children back, we have used a God gift box, in which as the retreat proceeds, the group members give up their excuses and burdens and give them to God to handle.

Our groups and seminars ALL start with an introduction, whether on a name tag, or out loud in a breakaway group, EVERYONE is asked to say this simple phrase. "My name is_ , I am wonderful because our Creator made me," We ask each participant to stand up in front of the group, or in the talking circle, read this sentence and tell us something wonderful and unique about themselves.

As discussed below, we do NOT require that anyone believe in our idea of a Creator, or any one religious practice or belief. We do however discuss that like breath, it does not matter, over the centuries and centuries of humans on this earth, without breath, we can NOT live, and our position is that without a faith in something (even if, like Bill Maher, it is a faith that there IS no God) we each NEED some kind of belief to uphold us when times are great, to thank that entity, or when times get hard, to lean upon. Even the staunchest of atheists needs a community of like believers to trust and lean on when the time comes, and to celebrate with when the sun comes up and they are still breathing. Most old old old people (like us) know. It is a gift to be grateful for to have one more day. NO MATTER WHAT.

# PERSONAL STORY

This story is in small part the reason for writing this book: There are many other parts in other books.

One day, driving in a borrowed vehicle, mine had been totally destroyed by two drunks racing, and they said it was MY fault, the one who stayed at the scene, rather than hit and run as his palsy did, had my same insurance company. The company said, we just found a great way for us to not have to pay anyone, we will find you both equally at fault, you have to pay your own damages. It also led to almost six years before an MRI was paid for by Social Security (I had retired by then and had full retirement Social Security that paid for any condition, and did NOT argue that auto insurance, either mine, or the drunks should pay for care). It was found the reason my legs were not able to move was they had bone injuries, combined with arthritis in the untreated conditions, and I needed a hip replacement. Due to the long years of not being treated my back and other leg, and all the muscles and soft tissue were injured enough to keep me still working on crutches and braces to learn to walk again, almost eight years later. Kind of hard for a horse trainer and equine therapist. I have not given up.

My sister Eva, and my sister (in law) Judith had died of cancer, leaving their teen and college age children without mothers, as well as two broken men to raise children alone. My Mom and Dad had passed away, from old age, expected, both were in hospice care, but still, a hard blow.

AND having found out the research levels of radiation that had saved my life from deadly stage four, level four cancer had just been diagnosed as the cause of internal bleeding.

The doctors sadly said, we told you when you volunteered for the research that we "might" be able to give you an extra two years, and we have more than done that, but we have no treatment for the radiation caused internal bleeding. I prayed for an answer. A friend with breast cancer, with implants that kept being rejected and having surgery after surgery told me she had been referred to a wonderful Osteopath and nutritionist who had helped her begin to heal. I went, saying to myself, I do not care if he says eat pebbles or marbles, I will do it and heal. He said eat overcooked rice, a zucchini and green been parsley soup put through the blender, and steamed fish to help the radiation burned intestines heal. A big treat, once in awhile meal was overcooked oatmeal and a few organic blueberries to make sure no chemicals were eaten on either the berries or the oats. Ten months into this hard to keep program, I asked him if I could eat a piece of home made angel cake, and some whipped cream and a strawberry or two for my birthday. He was surprised that I was still on the nutrition program, and that much still keeping to the program. I was sent for a colonoscopy. I had healed. I did not have to return for ten years for a follow up. Thank God, but that too had been a huge stress in many different ways.

AND we were looking for a new stable for our equine therapy program because a jerk with a flowers in his hair and his old hippie friends had taken over the ranch we had rented part of.........I was truly upset.

I had spent over $35,000 of my own money, borrowed and paid back $30,000 from friends and family, and had a student debt of $73,000 to earn a PhD. IF I had stayed at Cal Tech/ La Verne where I started while employed in a science project I would have had less or no student debt, and gotten my degree. BUT I had what turned out to be cancer and was bedridden, so went to online. What a mistake. The promised ADA Brain damaged support mentor was not there, and the final thousands of dollars to get a writer and editor were NOT covered as they had promised and would have been at Cal Tech/La Verne where I started my work in Reassessing and Restructuring Public Agencies. I had completed ALL my work, with a 3.74 average, even with APA deductions on each paper, and even without the promised statistics ADA aide. I had just found out the husband of our Senator owned the fraudulent lending company so got NO help from her when I asked. The State of course had listed the school with a top rating when I had checked it BEFORE enrolling. It was later found that it was a fraud, and we were told we would get class action repayments and our loans forgiven. LUCKILY the drunks racing hit me, and put me worse disabled and the loans were charged off due to the injuries ending my work. Except for almost ten thousand in loans from a bank I had not been told were NOT on my Federal Student loan program. A PhD without the final paper is useless.

Depressed.

I was driving along, and said, to our Creator (being Native American) I need a sign.

Somewhat like the movie Bruce Almighty, I turned the corner, and there, leaned against a trashcan, was a BEAUTIFUL sign. I could see the people had had a big party, as many trash cans were filled with pink tablecloths, and surrounded by pink tablecloths tied around the left overs and big black trash bags filled with party things. I knew the lady who owned the house briefly. I stopped and stared at the sign.

One day I had seen her Christmas decorations blowing off the fences and shrubs and down the street. I stopped to help her get them back. We stood on the truck bed of my four wheeler to put them back more securely.

One day I had seen her trying to get oranges off her trees, and again had stopped to help, the kids and we jumped up in the truck bed and got the oranges. I knew she would not mind my taking that sign on the street outside her trashcans.

I thought, unlike Bruce, I am going to heed this sign and took it up to my stable. The sign read..........

# .....*happily ever after*......

I thought this is JUST what I need.

I put the sign up and everyone who saw it, wanted one. We told the kids and the veterans, and the first responders and their families, as well as our volunteers to make their own posters, signs, and shirts with these words on them. We began to teach classes in probation and lock downs, in veteran groups, to single Mothers. Make your own poster, sign and/or shirt as the groups talked about their dreams, and their disappointments and began their own workbooks on rebuilding, or building a life in which they could live "happily ever after.....".

We found another stable, and what a nightmare. We ended up suing the city over an overzeaolous and/or corrupt animal control officer and moved to another COUNTY. Long story, it is in our book about equine therapy.

In the meantime one of our Board members died of MS. Our Director finally got her MRI from being assaulted by a student who should NOT have been in a public school, and it turned out to be a blessing, they found newly beginning spinal cord cancer and she had two surgeries, added to the surgeries she needed after being assaulted by the student.

The animal control Gestapo (as our lawyer called her when filing papers)was calling her in the intensive care unit, saying she BETTER get out and deal with her or go to jail. She could NOT reach me, because, as life will sometimes do, my cell carrier was putting in a new system and merging with another larger company and we could NOT use our cell phones. I did NOT use a home phone, I was always with the horses or doing a free seminar for high risk youth, veterans, and first responders and their families. We were paying $12,000 a month for a rented stable, and the staff to live in the house and care for the horses. One of them was a professional rodeo champion and owned her own horses, and her friend had helped her with her horses for years. Both the Director and I raised our own funds, and used our own disability and retirement payments to do this work. I closed my teachers retirement account to pay for the move and deposits to get the horses into the sanctuary and safe, after the events mentioned below. I have paid each month to keep the horses safe, letting the veteran run stable utilize them for their veteran and youth programs. These were all trained therapy horses in different levels of training and capabilities. This is discussed in another book.

We found a new stable, and moved every thing we had. Not more than two or three hours after unloading, a fast moving forest fire changed direction due to winds, and in less than 30 minutes the fire passed so rapidly every thing was burned, the steel bars warped, some of the welds melting out. The aluminum bars and covers burned, bent, along with the sheds, tack, feed, and office and garden items. ALL gone. Again, luckily, the woman driving the big stock trailers to bring the horses had called to say she had to get on a plane, family emergency in another state and did not move them that day. SO, the horses ALL were safe in their old stable, just all together, we had taken all the pens, arenas, and round corrals. The small animals had been taken by car and truck to another therapy program, so they too were safe. Of course the over zealous Gestapo woman wrote us up for the horses being in a huge lot, rather than stalls as well.

The sign had been in my friend's car, and left off at my home. There it was, each day, **....happily ever after.....** By then two more Board members had had severe health issues and moved away to family members states for care and love.

The State had investigated the by then long ago vehicle accident, so slowly that their report, that said the TWO racing drunks who hit me had been going over 80 mph when they hit my big fourwheeler, turning it to junk did not come until the statute of limitations had gone, so claimed the insurance company. I had to keep paying off the contract, since the insurance company had found both parties equally guilty.......
and the Statute of Limitations had run to sue the company So much for being there! Luckily I only owed a few more months

on the contract. The credit union was very surprised and happy that I did just pay off the contract on a totaled vehicle.

In the meantime I had received a recall notice on the truck, which said it would take off on its own when the brake was released. I called and said, well, it's a little late, the truck is totaled and the guys who hit me said the truck had jumped out at them, and months before I had gotten a ticket for the truck taking off across a six lane roadway FAST when I released the brake, right in front of a cop with a radar gun. I had to pay for traffic school, and the traffic school teacher had been super sick with a long lasting flu which I was fortunate to get. They said NO problem, we are going to take care of it, sent an email application, and two years later a snotty lawyer said, OH, you should not have believed us, you should have filed a lawsuit. Even though they were my favorite vehicle, I will never buy a Toyota again.

So, I needed my sign.

# ….. "happily ever after".

I was, for a little while since putting the horses in a safe ranch, loaned to another therapy program to reduce my costs to keep them alive, sitting on the couch, with Joyce and Joel, and other inspirational speakers of many religions looping over and over on my cable recordings. And going to my own church at least twice a week. One day my older son said "you know Mom, you have to eat". I said "I am doing the best I can". We both laughed. I looked at my sign and went off to help care for our Director who had just gotten out of hospital. I had to take two busses and walk on crutches and braces to get up to her house, but she was not doing so well, even with an everyday nurse dropping by.

We said, ... **"happily ever after"** and decided to hang on and reorganize and get restarted. The project "48 Acres" described below, was left hanging in a day when the Governor, to make himself look great for reducing costs to the state, canceled and closed the State Redevelopment Agency that had ASKED us to donate our time and experience as a team to design and develop the project expected to provide services to more than 70,000 returning Afghan and Iraq veterans and their families. They were kind enough to tell our group of retired old persons that we could buy the land donated by the city and provide the building and services ourselves. More on that below, and in another book. WE began to look for ways to facilitate for our expected clients to live "happily ever after..." and help each other.

WE ourselves, over the decades had to stop and make up our minds to live "happily ever after", and we want to share our concept as we once again embark on our vision to build three tiered treatment and housing programs with and for veterans, first responders, and high risk youth and their families. SO, we decided to choose to live happily ever after, and share that with others. That is what this book is about.

9

MADE in the USA

WE are Americans. We believe if a person is a Native, NOT a several generation immigrant, but a Native, or a born in America American, or a visitor or immigrant there is a clear responsibility to know the laws, and keep them. To know history and how America came about, even the genocide of the original people. Reality is real, if we lie, and pretend, we are NOT going to make America what it is intended to be, a nation of states run by THE people, FOR the people and BY the people.

The hardest part of writing a book that wants to facilitate for others to find their vision, their passion, their path on a road to meet their own dreams is, finding a title that will inspire the people you need to read the book, WANT to read it. The next hard part is finding a way to say what is needed to facilitate for others to WANT to find their way.

This book is a first step. A baby step. Many programs are discussed in this book. These are programs, books, videos that have helped each member of our Board, and each of our clients over the years. We thank those who have often given free, or low cost services (some of the books for self success can be purchased online for so little the $3.50 shipping charge is many times the price of the used book). On this subject, as with many diet, or exercise programs the success often rests in opening the book and READING it I was given the blessing of a free hour with a $750 an hour life coach, he recommended

Canfield's Success Principles. He said, read the book all the way through. Go back and re-read the book, put questions in the margins, put tabs on the pages, and THEN go back a third time and start the exercises. I have purchased used books for my program participants, and found many of the books, for one little penny, had few, if any marks in the books, some were even signed, someone paid to go to a seminar, and did not use the books as directed in the book itself. I am sure there are people who said, "that program, I tried it, it did not work".

We recommend joining a group online, in a community center, or start one yourself to give yourself support and inspiration to reach your goals. One lady had wanted for decades to start a national Native American story-sharing project. By the time she finally started it, in ONE WEEK she had over 15,000 followers, every person who read the site, shared it and brought in others. Who knew? In a book writing group several of the starting members, just by finding one or two other authors in their own interest area, and thousands to support them, have written a long wished for book in less than a year.

One of our biggest inspirations is parent groups that figure out what their schools need, and raise funds, have barn raisings, and get those things. A school with 5,000 students, no matter how poor, can find out how much an Olympic set of diving and swimming pools costs, and begin to recruit a team to dig, build, and help. Often Habitat for Humanity and local community support building programs can help you find people who will donate time, machines, and expert workers to put in pools, sports fields, stands, and gyms. One group found a huge concrete company that had to clean out their trucks daily, it actually helped them, besides giving them a tax write off, to have each of the trucks stop by the build site and have a group of trained volunteers put in prepared set areas for many projects. A win win, no more cement to pay to get rid of, and no cost for the cement for several jobs for the parent inspired programs.

RAISING, or BECOMING

To raise children takes a village, to allow a monster to just grow, takes no interest. (Research has been completed to show that just ONE adult, in a few hours here and there, a teacher, principal, or coach, friend's parent, can make a lifelong difference in the life of a child). To facilitate for a child to "become" their own best, is HARD, it will be discussed in this book. Yet, it is easy, as each member of the village finds and takes their part in raising these good earth citizens.

Mention must be made here that just one rotten adult, or another warped youth can destroy the lives of many young people. We feel it merits mentioning that every young person needs many in the village to help them steer clear of, and heal from these bad influences.

Let's raise all our nation and global children to **live happily ever after!!!**

# HOW, to "live happily ever after...."

There are many stages to living happily ever after, but the most important one, the first one is to DECIDE you are going to live happily ever after, and find out how to do that NO MATTER WHAT.

Most, if not ALL of the great religious and cultural leaders of history have told us, to make up our minds to live happily NO MATTER WHAT. Find one that fits your thoughts and states of mind. Read the history, watch documentaries of the history of religions, and it is easy to see that what the original PERSON said has been, like the children's game of telephone, changed from each person telling the story and making up the rules. Most religions and psychology, the secular child of Freud to help humans stop their suffering, lose their fears, and "find" God or "not God" as they can are the same, all flawed, but this does not mean the world, or it's Creator are flawed.

A Rabbi I studied with started three temples, he was thrown out of his own temples sooner or later by rich benefactors who did NOT like what he taught, and wanted to find and hire a rabbi who would do what THEY wanted, not what was best for themselves or the people of that community. My law office was visited by an ancient woman, a survivor of Auschwitz Concentration Camp, her entire family gone, husband, children siblings, parents, grandparents, she was being evicted from her apartment. ALL of her assets had been given to a religious old person home, her husband (also a Concentration Camp survivor who had lost everyone) had not realized only HIS life was in the contract of the home. All the hundreds of thousands of dollars they had earned in a chain of deli restaurants they built over the years went to the home, but when he passed, they cold heartedly threw her out. My lead attorney said to me, help her out, no charge. We got her an extension and a cash settlement from the new owner who wanted to remodel the building. It ran out, we had found no help from any holocaust supporting community group or Temple. I took her home as my Aunt had recently moved to a city nearer to her daughter, daughter in laws, and grandchildren. I too was moving, and HAD to find her a place. I finally found a great social worker with elder services for the County who got her into a senior home. The only Rabbi to visit her was the one that had lost his Temples to rich benefactors who thought their money bought them the right to demand how those Temples were run. A sad lesson to me in religions. Find a religion who actually supports and helps their members. Every televised religious program advises people to find a local religious site to belong to. My thought is to shop around, and be part of the community if they let you. If they do not, find a new place to explore until you find home base, to give, and to receive from as needed.

There was a group named by fraud investigators "church gorillas" who would come in, criticize and divide the members, and take over the church, temple, mosque, or community center (recently a woman was arrested for defrauding an area Girl Scout program of its combined funds from many troops) until they took over the money and left the church, temple, or mosque without assets it had built up over the decades. A friend of mine divorced her husband when she found out that slick lawyer that he was, he had done that to our church, making a LOT Of money for himself and his friends, leaving others to struggle to fix the holes in the roof, and care for the community that had donated all the money to build those assets.

I was working on an interfaith project to build love and harmony between religions and people of America, several rabbis, priests and pastors told me they could NOT ask their membership to attend any of the round table educational exchanges because the little group of cronies would not let them. They would get fired. I am sure that the people in religious organizations do NOT go there to have political fights, yet a part of belonging, to a family, even to your own life, is to address conflict and stand up to it. Sometimes you just have to make up your mind to either leave, or help address the conflict and deal.

Most of us need community, and have to learn how to stand up for it. From Twelve Step programs to any faith group, or community program each of us has to learn to identify these situations and how to deal with them. Go out and join reading groups, community program support programs, or just get a group together and knit, crochet, or quilt tiny blankets for children around the world that are being born and wrapped in newspapers, because their Mothers do not have the means to give them even a welcome blanket to this world. MANY Scouting programs do this type of project both globally, and raise funds and make blankets (boys and girls, learning to sew is a skill we all need, one of my sons earned a LOT of extra money in his teen years by getting his school friends to donate jeans they had outgrown. He made purses and skirts out of them, and sold them to girls who had crushes on the owners of the pants). Whether at someone's house, the park, a community center, sitting around talking and sewing, sharing someone's sewing machine and skills helps make a person learn to live "happily ever after". Police departments, Paramedics and Fire Fighters as well as Social Workers and even Judge's for Children's Services Departments ALL need nice new special blankets and huggy toys for children they pick up in accidents and remove from homes where the parents are arrested, injured, or have the children removed due to abuse and/or neglect.

Go out and visit community groups, religious groups, talk to people and find just the right place for YOU to have support on the days it is HARD to live happily ever after NO MATTER WHAT. One of my friends had amazing remote control cars, construction sets and vehicles that he had received as gifts as a child, he took them to foster care group homes and lock downs and helped the children and youth design tracks, and construction sites. Many of those children and teens have gone on to college and trade schools and become architects, city designers, and construction workers and been recruited into the military to set up in country base sites from special training based on their interest grown from those happy days in the dirt of their group home.

One of our rodeo champion friends used her own show trailer, and rodeo champion horses to take to project sports fields. She was awesome, leading every person who wanted a ride, from the oldest Grandparent, to the youngest child, on one of her horses and letting them take pictures. The probation officers had discounts at pizza restaurants, and purchased amazing pizza for those at these events to teach about animals, and the need for environmental preservation of wild life migratory paths and waterways, as well as help to raise funds for world wildlife projects protecting wild life and protecting them from extinction and poaching. These programs were offered free to private schools as well. Many of those young girls, then teen age show pony owners, and champions now own their own equine therapy programs and work with others to restore wild horse lands and spaces for free roaming wild horse and burros around the world.

One day a Pastor from the church I had grown up in when at my Grandparents or on my Mom time after my parents divorce and we kids had joined the back and forth marathon of divorced children who have the joy of going back and forth from home to home on court scheduled visits, came to visit me when I was in the hospital waiting for surgery.

He remarked that I had admirable courage, he had never seen me afraid. I laughed to myself, I was one of the world's most fearful persons, I felt, but had parents who taught us that bravery is not the reality of not being afraid, it was the act of doing what had to be done NO MATTER how great the fear.

Whether you have a preferred religious background, or like world famous atheist Bill Maher find your strength, kindness and concern for the earth and other humans where it is he finds it I feel that each of us needs to build a faith system for ourselves.

Truthfully, I am sure the Creator of the long long long standing universe does not have any concern with our tiny earthling beliefs, words, or ideas of what ALL is ALL about. Native children all over the world, if raised in their own cultures are trained from earliest days from birth that the Creator of ALL does not need, nor want OUR help to run the universe, and is there for us to guide, and encourage and strengthen us, NO MATTER what, so be calm, live in peace and harmony with nature and leave the God-doing to God.

I still find it important for each person to find and join a community that supports and helps each person get through hard times, and be led forward in despairing times, and to help others when fortunate enough to be in the position to do so.

It harms my heart that THE major cause of hate, distrust, war and violence in the world and in history has been religion. NOT the Creator of ALL, but humans gathering in little groups to hate and harm each other in their name for their idea of a supreme being.

Bob Dylan wrote a song (With God on Our Side) reminding us that we humans love to do bad things and claim God is on Our Side. Michner wrote in the book Hawaii that the religious came to the Hawaiian Islands to lighten the load of the Hawaiian Natives. He alleges they did a great job, they took not just everything but the kitchen sink, as the old saying goes, but the sink and the house and land it was attached to as well.

The most important step in finding a way to live "happily ever after" is to find a peace and harmony with the universe and the Creator of ALL, whatever that means to each one of us.

Talking to people from various religions from time to time, I said, to myself, if I am wrong, and God is only what you say, then at the end of this life for me, I will have had a good, productive, and FUN life, and when I asked for a sign, got one that said "happily ever after" I have lived happily. If I do not go to a place with angels, and gold streets, and have to learn to play a harp, then I am not going to be overwhelmingly sad. I have a hard enough time with THIS life and have no desire to attempt to figure out what about the before, or the after. Yet, if I am right, and you are wrong, you have spent your life making yourself and others try to live up to a life that there is NO real proof God wants us to live.

Each of us has to make up our own mind as to how to relate, or not relate to God or a higher wisdom than ours. I do however feel it is necessary to living happily ever after to find a peace and harmony with God (or no God if you are an atheist).

I have been fortunate to grow up in a culturally mixed family and with family members who like other people and love to enjoy and learn about those they meet. I enjoy holidays and celebrations and learning about them with others. Rather than fight with, or put others down for their ways of life, I have found it grounding and expanding to respect and learn about the ways of others. My Mom's Jewish friends came to my Grandmother's home to celebrate Christmas, and we made sure to have them help us choose, and accept Kosher foods so they would be able to keep their dietary customs. We went to their Temple, and homes, for celebrations and holidays. Our family has members of many different religions, celebrating together and learning and respecting each other has led to a lot of happiness for us all. One of my closest Jewish friends, a Rabbi, told me that people need to realize it is NOT about dishes, it is about humane and sanitary treatment of animals used for food resources. People need to know their own religions and stop using their religion to build hate and divisiveness. We, as humans NEED to do this in order to "live happily ever after...".

I have found that extremes do have some good points. Sometimes we do NOT agree with people, and I certainly have a more accepting attitude and believe in respecting other people. However, I also have found that by talking to, and respecting the opinions of others, I have learned things, and also feel that sometimes someone completely opposed to my beliefs is a good place to check myself on how I live my life. AM I too self evaluating, and do things that maybe I need to reconsider. I have learned often that mean treatment as children by others different from themselves has led to a lifetime of anger and hatred NOT to those who abused them, but to the whole of a people similar to those persons.

Being self righteous is a great way to make sure you do NOT live "happily ever after". I have also found, in my work with criminals that many people have a culture that I disagree with strongly that harms themselves and others, and often am able to open a gateway to their seeing a kinder way of life. Sometimes to seek help to deal with addictions of many types. Ted Bundy, the serial killer, his lawyers revealed, wanted first offenders to know that both drugs and pornography are addictions that can lead to the horror of having an addiction to killing. PHEW. It is easy to hate the person rather than the actions, and to not learn how to prevent the horrors of criminal action. Helping others to live "happily ever after" can help make the lives of the victims they do NOT have much easier to live happily ever after.

I surely had NO goal of learning that, or changing my career goals while listening to a prestigious law professor in my Crimes classes at law school tell us about the reality of criminal law and some of the notorious criminals he had represented. He also taught us that lawyers are there to defend the RIGHTS, not the wrongs of their clients. Learn, who knows what you will learn that will not only help YOU live happily ever after, but help others to LIVE happily ever after. Much more on this subject later in this book, and in my book "BIG LIZ, THE LEADER OF THE GANG", a book about my work in gang abatement.

Now that you have found GOD (or not) it is time to learn to live happily ever after with yourself.

This includes simple things like a balanced life of sleep, work, recreation, relationships, and getting rid of addictions that will keep you from living happily ever after. From over eating, to under eating, drugs, shopping, gossip, busy body activities (there is a great difference and distance between care and concern to others, and an attempt to control and manipulate others), hoarding, whether animals, things, or too many activities, cleaning, or not cleaning, exercise (yes, I knew people who were beyond annoying with their attempts to keep calories flowing, doing pushups, or jumping jacks while attempting to talk to others) hypochondriacs, or those addicted to being sad sacks. Many people need just a hand to get going again, others are addicted to being needy (there are new classes being taught about the "culture" of poverty of certain groups of persons. As with any other addiction, some people need help to deal with their addiction to poverty and lack.

## SELF

Simple things such as sleep are often hard work. Yet as with most problems, may have simple solutions. There are books, meditations, and groups along with professional counselors who specialize in learning how to sleep. One of the simple solutions is whether it is a tent on a street corner, or a massive double California King bed in a mansion, to set aside a place to SLEEP and get yourself to know, lay down here, and SLEEP.

Nutrition and health. Many people have real health problems. Some doctors are now suggesting, and it is in the book on food and weight control by Dr. Phil McGraw that the balance of the body actually can make one person eat less and not be able to lose weight. Some doctors suggest that endocrine problems are the cause, not the result of weight gain. No matter what, it is up to YOU to learn your own body, and how to keep it nourished and healthy as possible. To care for your body, whether sick or well, starts with YOU.

Mental health. If you do not feel happy, relaxed, comfortable in your life, learn how to handle life better. This also is not easy, but there are seminars, books, and professional counselors who help others learn how to keep life balanced, no matter what. Some people are ready and eager to "cast their burdens" as the Bible tells us Jesus requested. To leave the stress to God, and do what we can at the moment to deal sensibly with any issue. The movie "Beautiful Life" in which a man manages to sneak his young son into hiding, right in a concentration camp, and gets others in the camp to make a goal, a game of keeping the boy alive and not found allows the boy to be kept alive and survive the camps. The father manages to make his son live through the horror of the loss of his Mother and eventually even his Father gives a great inspiring message of living happily ever after. The books by Native Americans who survived the horrors of the death marches and the trail of tears being forced off their lands and shuffled here and there to concentration camps also inspire. Mental health is surviving life without becoming so broken you harm yourself or others in the myriad of ways broken humans harm themselves and others. It is a necessary step for anyone who wants to live happily ever after.


## HOME

Once a person has found their own happily ever after state, it is now a question of how to share it with family, or room mates, or work mates to expand how much happily ever after can be shared.

## DO NOT BE MISLED.

Some people do not like YOU. It hurts until you realize no one gets liked by everyone, and a lot of people over the centuries have harmed their own lives by trying to make sure EVERYONE approves of them. Learning to accept those who do not like you, even if it is close family, or a long term friend who has changed is part of living happily ever after.

The Aesop Fable about the man who was leading his little donkey down the road, both enjoying their walk is a great learning story. The man and donkey were happy, until a man came up and said, how stupid, ride the donkey....so the man mounted up, and then saw a woman who said, you stupid abusive man, riding than tiny animal, you should carry him, so he struggled to carry both the packages the donkey had once been happily carrying, as well as the donkey. He came upon a man who said, what an idiot, make that donkey walk and carry your packages. The donkey had had enough, struggled, and knocked the man into the creek with his packages and ran off home.

We can all learn to do what is enjoyable and happy, and NOT listen to the critics who have NOTHING to do with what we are doing.

This does NOT mean to allow people to abuse animals, or to not listen if someone asks us kindly to consider a different position than our own, but it does mean each of us needs to learn to live happily ever after without trying to satisfy everyone else.

Television, Movies, Music Videos, magazines, and just about everyone has some trendy idea they attempt to push off on us ALL the time. It is up to us to learn the reality, people want YOU to buy their things, so THEY can make more money, not any positive reason or concern for YOUR living happily ever after. It is up to us to learn that if we want to mow lawns, or work at a fast food chain, and live in our parent's basement to buy an expensive sports car that we can not legally drive over the top speed limit of 70 mph in most states, that is up to us, NOT someone else. And if we have a mansion, and want to drive an old thirties pick up truck with the ground visible below the pedals because the running boards long decades ago fell out, it is up to us, NOT someone else to make those decisions.

Yet, there are many fun toys in technology that help us have fun in our day-to-day lives. Learning to live happily ever after means to learn to balance and accept your own choices in these areas. Learning to do this in your own family and home is an important step to living happily ever after.

BUT, this does not mean put on your scraggly muddy shorts you have had since high school gym class, and oldest flip flops and go get mad because a black tie restaurant or hotel does NOT want you there. This does NOT mean go to the ball game and get into fights with people wearing the other team's shirt, or hat.

This means to learn to get along with people, to respect them, and their choices rather than to use anything that is not YOU as an excuse to bully, abuse or in other ways (gossip, back stab, call city officials, tell the teacher, etc) because YOU are in fact a mean and critical person who has not learned how to manage your own negative emotions.

# "happily ever after..."

means to learn to do active positive things to create change, it does NOT mean to sit around with a group of griping people listing everything that is wrong and what we would do if a lot of stingy people or the taxpayers, would just give us the money to get paid to do what we have decided is best. Helping our block or community live happily can help us to live happily ever after if we know how to do this in a positive way, and not stress out trying to make it all better on our own, or expecting everyone to like OUR way.

In mediation programs it used to be taught how to get everyone on the same page, to create positive change. Today, mediation is often a way to make sure no one ever gets to a place of resolution of problems and issues.

Example: If you go to a family counselor, and the sessions start with what is WRONG, rather than asking each person to prepare a one or two minute presentation of what each person wants to see happen in a positive way, it is much more likely that positive change will begin to be achieved.

Yet, it is important to hear what is bothering people. In Mediation this can be brought to the table by asking each person what they WANT and what they NEED in the situation. Each person is given a small amount of time to present their thoughts on the issues. A child or teen may say "I want the family to get along", this might be changed to I NEED the family to stop fighting and tearing me apart. Being positive does NOT mean one has to avoid or ignore or not address negative issues. YOU make me sick is not the same message as I feel torn apart and alone when you two continue to fight and argue and blame in front of me, and the other children. Then each person is asked what THEY can do to create those positive changes to begin.

There was a Priest who wrote a book titled "Pictures from the Heart" in which he put pictures drawn by children who were in divorce and/or custody proceedings. One child drew a picture of a child, with barbed wire wrapped around her heart, her parents each had an end of the barbed wire and were pulling it as hard as they could.

In our project "Kids Anonymous", the teens and youth said, WE NEEDED this sooner, so THEY invented and implemented "Kids Jr". When new members were referred by therapists in the project, they would be asked to talk about themselves, led by the sentence, I am wonderful, GOD created me, and telling us something wonderful about themselves. It was as for all other programs, often very hard for a young person to say. How, we the adults, the professionals, wondered, did we destroy the perfect gifts from God given to our village, our earth. Next the kids would ask about their family, as they began to tell the kids what was going on, the kids would say, OHHH, wisely, your parents are pills.

My Grandmother had used the word pill for us when we were being disruptive and making her life miserable. The children asked us what a pill was, and thought it sounded like their parents, grandparents, and often lawyers and counselors. The new member of the group always got raging mad, and would yell at the others to not call their parents pills. Then they would stop, and say, what is a pill. The members would laugh and say, OH you know, and list things they ALL had gone through. Is your Mom/Dad still seeing that (expletive), or did your Father give you my check? The favorites were the name calling and gossip done to friends and family as if the child or teen was not standing right there, and the best, OH, you are growing up just like HIM/HER and deciding one parent would take one child, the other the other, as if they were shoes being divided by a Court. By this time the new member would be laughing and say, OH YES, they are pills.

The other members said, we learn how to let them do their thing, and stay out of it. Such wisdom from young people, the therapists would take the responsibility to deal with the parents and lawyers. One of the psychiatrists who trained many of the therapists and development specialists told us, you just write it up, I will deal, YOU do not have the power and the money to tell these parents what they need to hear. AND she told us, she had the court mandate to tell the JUDGE what was needed to be heard. These were all Court mandated custody cases. The work was offered to the community for FREE by the Psychiatrists and therapists who utilized students who actually PAID to come and do internships and learn the most heartbreaking part of therapy work, family case work.

As discussed below, in 48 Acres, these programs were included in the plans for family support for veterans. Some programs were Court Mandated programs for women veterans who had lost custody of their children due to PTSD related violence. Some of the women veterans had voluntarily given up custody due to their own ability to see they were dangerous to their children in their present untreated condition. Both male and female veterans were in the Court Mandated programs for domestic violence, having assaulted their spouses, children, parents, siblings caring for the children and even grandparents caring for the children. The heartbreaking stories kept on coming. Whole families murdered by one or the other PTSD untreated veteran. Often BOTH parents had untreated PTSD. The stories of untreated PTSD veterans who killed themselves in the house with spouse and / or children helped us to go out and get donations, and spend our own money to provide free programs to the families. Often those successful families referred other families, and also helped at our fundraising events to make sure the programs were there for other hurting families.

The veterans themselves telling us that they could NOT get treatment because they were immediately listed as mentally ill, put on expensive medications that made them into zombies, and could no longer have a dream of any life as many careers, including ongoing military careers where closed to them. We BEGGED five Presidential Administrations to address this issue, we were rarely graced with a form letter thanking us for our thoughts, telling us our representatives have many things to address and this was not important enough to be addressed and resolved immediately.

YOUNG veterans began to tell us that even though they had been recruited with promises of training, education and career chances they were instead sent to boot camp, and into combat, and for one reason or another let go. They were NOT considered veterans. Their families, even if they were severely injured in combat, were given thirty day notice to get out of military housing, if they had qualified for housing in the first place. Base commanders, when our Director went to discuss lack of housing for veterans, said, "VETERANS", our active duty are sleeping in their cars and under bridges.

That problem was "addressed" by a few warehouses and barracks being opened into cots in mass housing for those waiting to be redeployed. Their families on wait lists living with parents, friends, or homeless.

Several congresspersons, on both sides of the aisles attempted to address these issues, our Director and Board were invited to speak and present documentation at panels, and in a hearing in Wasington DC. Our Director paid with her own credit cards for the women veterans, and other veteran group members to get to Washington DC, she was never repaid. She paid for the hotels, plane fares, and food for those in the hearings.

What, we ask ourselves, is the significance of this to living "happily ever after". Each of us has to relate in a positive way to real life and resolve problems, NOT give just old clothes, and the food we cleaned out of the pantry and do not want, or the left over and off label food bought with the hundreds of millions of dollars donated to charities that "say" they are providing food for the hungry of our country. It is up to each of us to find out what is happening to the money we donate.

# GOOD EARTH CITIZENS

A good earth citizen is what YOUR view is, and living YOUR life with passion and joy, and yet, not harming others. The Dad who has a mid life crisis and runs off with his receptionist who is half his age harms his children. In the moment of their lives where they NEED to have a dream, and a dream of a life partner in this hard to navigate world of ours, his actions crush their dreams. How can we ask young people to believe in a life partner, who will be there for us, when the most important man in their life runs off with someone who loves his money, and is too lazy to go out and find her own life, or life partner to EARN the middle and elderly years of comfort. This is not just about men, that "urban" housewife, who pretends she is trendy, but in reality is just a part time prostitute while her husband and children are at work and school is not any better. Women who have affairs with men who want a married woman need to understand reality, these men go out with married women because they do NOT want a relationship, just sex, and it harms your children, along with your spouse. More on this subject in our book on good relationships and sexuality and how to teach these concepts to our children.

A good earth citizen is a person who does NOT harm other people, the air, water, earth, or the animals and other creatures on this earth. How can we reconcile our agencies and the reality of the world with this principle?

Texting, drinking, being on drugs, or putting others at risk while driving is NOT good earth citizenship. Stealing from other people, in person, online, or using your employees to do the stealing (of time, money, work, love and any other thing someone would not give you if you were honest) is NOT OK.

Allowing your children to be your passive aggressive toys to annoy those who you "think" are allowing you to "get even" for whatever it is you do not feel you "got" as a child, or teen is NOT OK.

Allowing others in your family, your job, your city, county, or State, or country to harm others is NOT OK.

More on these subjects will be discussed later in this book, or in other books.

Introduction to Good American citizenship. Legal or not here legally, people in America need to be VERY aware of the rights and responsibilities of every human upon the soils under the category of "America". Including military bases, and on vacation, you are representing America.

Hundreds of thousands of people want to come to America. WHY?

Many want money, not freedom. To BE a good citizen of this earth, it is necessary to know what it is to BE a good citizen. In America, we do NOT need revolutions, or divisions between the people. We have huge libraries filled with laws, and yet we are alleged to have more crime, more murders, and more deadly mass shootings than anywhere in the world except active war zones.

EVERYONE NEEDS to learn the real history of America, and as Native Americans have been forced to deal with, or be murdered, there WERE NO Native wars, just genocidal death marches. One was even named by Congress "THE Termination Bill of 1830". Allowing every treaty made with Native Nations across all American, Canadian, Alaskan and island lands to be broken, generally by murdering the people.

The original Euro-settlers were NOT as we have carefully been taught, people in search of religious freedom. YES, there was a group of people who wanted religious freedom, but sponsored by a Dutch shipping and trading company with the agreement that half of the land they stole from the Natives, would be given to those who sponsored them. Half of any profits they obtained from farming, forestry, killing the animals of those who owned those lands would be returned to the shipping company. The company then sent other groups. The people who had been living in civilized confederacies of over 800 Native Nations that stretched from the top of Alaska to the Southern tip of S. America, and ALL of the islands along both coasts were members of allied nations that belonged to that one confederacy that had learned many lessons over the thousands of years they had either lived on these soils, or come and obeyed the LAWS to become members of those societies.

The "first" Americans also brought slaves, indentured servants, and from the old shipping records large numbers of "adopted" children they bought from prisons to be a different kind of abused child labor slave to build homes, start farms, and do the hard work of starting businesses for those who came here.

A recent travel program on ABC noted in a tourist program about Ireland that the VIKINGS had settled there more than 6,000 years ago. Many of those VIKINGS traveled, traded and rode the seas in their amazing ships 2,500 years before Moses convinced the slaves to step into the Red Sea and be free! To say a group four hundred years ago "found" America, or any of the American and Alaskan, land, assets, or continents is plain and simply a lie. That same travel documentary lists an archaeological site that proves Ireland itself was long inhabited by people with the ability to at least carve caves, build walls, and farm using irrigation and selective replanting, they were not waiting with wonder and amazement to be raped, pillaged, and turned into slaves by the invading genocidal hordes that created a centuries long war that was supposed to have been "religious", it was not, it was caused by greed, genocide and avarice of invaders against the original citizens.

Again, when the Irish ship builders, and those kidnapped by ship crews and forced into labor as ship crew and mercenary soldiers (a documentary on old buildings was hunting for a reason as to why bars had a little hatch behind the bar, and found it was for when a person was too drunk, and passed out, no matter what their gender, class, financial situation, or ability when sober was tumbled down into a place where ship captains and crew gathering members would grab them, dump them in a room on the ship. When they awoke, they could either do as told, or walk that short plank!). While they were trading along many coasts, they often jumped ship, choosing to live among the native people rather than to continue the hard and dangerous life of a forced labor sailor and mercenary soldier. Cortez is said to have sunk his own ships to make sure his mercenary army did not try to mutiny when they found out what they were facing in their proposed genocide of the Inca, Maya, and Aztec nations.

As more and more of those who wanted money came, they also brought along the euro- self appointed leadership desires for empire building. Notably the Spanish, Portuguese and Russian empire builders met and divided up all the "unknown" lands and assets and sent along their soldiers, armed with recently invented guns, canons, and genocidal orders to take slaves and sell them from all who could work, and murder the rest of the citizens of the lands. IF in fact they thought the lands were unknown, and uninhabited, why did they order the genocide of all who would not work in THEIR best interests, or be threatened into slavery and sold.

The greedy empire builders fought wars between themselves constantly for the lands, and assets, both in their own countries, and around the world which they "drafted" soldiers in many ways to fight. Some of the nations had centuries of history of "raping and pillaging", and as they went along, all young men able to be forced into fighting were told be in the army, or we kill your family. Many young women were grabbed and forced into "camp prostitution" where they were raped repeatedly and either killed, or just left wherever the army passed along its route to the next village to rape and pillage, or to the next battle they were being forced marched to.

This practice continued for centuries. The Nazi Army, in its last death march across Europe is shown in the film series "The Real History of the World" by Oliver Stone. By coincidence, a small village had a festival on their last day on earth, film was taken and salvaged by video journalists who had moved on to another assignment. A quiet, happy village, filled with people obviously celebrating a holiday. Some hours later Allied troops moved into the village. All that was left was a smoldering church. The men and boys had been forced off as labor with the Nazi troops, by threats to their families. As soon as they were marched down the road, as was the usual custom, the clean up crew of Nazi troops left behind bulldozed down the homes, shops, and forced all those left, women, children, elderly, disabled into the church and set it on fire, burning everyone to death. ONE woman managed to crawl out a window after the blast of the fire blew the window out and escaped to the forest. When she was rescued by the Allied troops, she was horribly burned, but able to tell them what had happened between the early news video and the reality they found as they marched after the Nazi troops. The Bible itself tells of centuries of empire builders and those escaping their captors going along raping and pillaging, murdering those on the lands they wanted for themselves.

Human beings have to find a better way to live together.

# "happily ever after"

The American Revolution occurred when those who had escaped the empire builders for many reasons, had enough and decided to create a new vision for human governance. The stories of each of those who signed the Declaration of Independence are a mismatched hodgepodge of people who joined that vision and built the reality. Those signers knew, without doubt, that if they did not win that war, they would be hunted down, it would not be hard, their names were on the line of the document declaring independence. When found they would have been drawn and quartered, a civilized method of killing traitors. The person was tied to four horses, or four teams of horses and pulled to pieces by hitting the animals. BUT, not to death, they were saved for public hanging, their bodies burned, their ashes scattered in unknown places so no one could find them to honor or remember them.

Americans hoped to have found a better way to live together.

SOME of the Founders (the diaries, and newspaper letters and articles written by the Founders and those afraid to join, or those who were making too much money off the suffering of others are interesting to read, and all available through the Library of Congress) wanted these freedoms and rights for everyone, others wanted them for themselves, so they did not have to pay taxes and bow to empire builders far across the oceans. BUT they did not want them for their slaves, indentured servants, or child labor "adopted" orphans. The Constitution has allowed the PEOPLE to test the PEOPLE-ness of the Constitution and the nation to change and expand the rights to ALL people.

Today, we are currently in a war of words and building walls, protesting and using horrible conditions in other lands to justify and to argue either side of the issues. NO ONE has asked the Native Americans if they want MORE people here on THEIR lands. More on this issue in other books and in current documentaries being filmed from new archeological finds and research. No one asked the Native Americans if they wanted the FIRST groups of illegal immigrants here. Washington made treaties with the Native Americans if they helped him win his war for freedom, not one more Native life or Native acre would be taken "as long as the sun shone, and as long as the rain came down" forever. The Revolutionary troops would NOT have won without the Scouts, clothing, food and moccasins as well as horses for their troops. Yet, in 1830, a greedy, corrupt Congress wrote THE TERMINATION Bill of 1830 giving themselves permission and money to wipe out the rest of the Native Nations across the continents and islands of America, and steal the lands and assets. They had found out it was hard to enslave the Native Nations because they, unlike the African slaves or indentured servants from Europe, KNEW where they were and how to get to safety and freedom and ran off as soon as they saw an opening. Many of the original founding families and communities of America did NOT believe anyone was allowed to be treated unequally, or unfairly.

Those people

WE as a HUMAN RACE have to help each other build these rights for EVERYONE, EVERYWHERE to live **"happily ever after"**.

Mexicans were the citizens of many of the Southwestern States of the United States. We will discuss the real history of these lands, including the NAZI war criminal prisoners in some Southwest States and Alaska who Senator McCarthy and old Joe Kennedy let go. More on this in Truman's biography, and the book "McCarthy, THE Most Hated Senator EVER". IF immigrants are to be thrown out, it should be those who escaped NAZI prison camps and their spouses, children and other descendents and family members who came to America in some of those "chains" of family members after World War II. How do we as a nation justify keeping out, or throwing out those who actually owned these lands when the French and others "decided" to sell them to England???? France and other illegal immigrants and genocidal maniacs did not EVER declare war on the Native Americans. Instead they brought in newly invented guns, canons, and mercenary troops and came in the midnight, or created treaties with people who had no authority to make those treaties, then broke them and stole the land by murder, torture, and killing off the forests, prairies, waters, and animals owned by the Native Nations.

The history of America itself is one of genocide, there were NO guns and NO wars with Native American NATIONS. More than often the "wars" consisted of one or two greedy persons such as Hearst in California who PAID bounty hunting mercenaries for each SCALP, man, woman, child of the Native Nation citizens so HE and his palsies could take the land and assets. Even the Spanish land grant families were not freed of the greed and avarice of these land barons, cattle barons, and mining, lumber and eventually industrial company owners in Native Nations George Washington had promised would never be touched, and would be protected by the United States of America. The treaties had such flowery words as "until the sun ceases to shine" or "until the rain ceases to fall".

Whether a Native American, a several generations family nationalized citizen of the United States, or a visitor, or immigrant, legal or illegal, every human on American soil needs to know the Rights and Responsibilities of being a good citizen in America under the Constitution.

The Ten Rights and Responsibilities of the United Nations were formed from the Constitution of the United Nations and taught globally for many decades. First Lady Eleanor Roosevelt recognized the need to spread the Constitution without empire building. The books and documentaries about her and the United Nations NEED to be mandatory for every young person on earth.

The Constitution in America has failed to teach the Rights, and the Responsibilities of every human on American soils, waters, and air space.

The book Reassessing and Restructuring Public Agencies, 2017, Wiley) contains those Rights, and the Responsibilities along with suggestions for finding classes and books, or online information to be a good world and good American citizen, even if just a tourist for a few days. Our programs all utilize the workbooks for the programs to teach each human on earth their rights, and the accompanying responsibilities of being a good earth citizen.

The Constitution: To start study for a child, or new arrival to America the Constitution needs to be understood, it gives RIGHTS, but demands RESPONSIBILITIES. Most people know all the singers and their album offerings, or actors and all their marriages and divorces, or the athletic or dance skills and awards for many celebrities, but do not know the basic laws and supportive history of the United States of America.

The history of the United States:

The reality of each town, berg, county, state and our country.

WHY do other people want to come to America???? Understanding the RESPONSIBILITIES of coming to America.

# TEN RIGHTS AND RESPONSIBLITIES OF THE UNITED NATIONS

The United Nations building is founded in New York City, in the State of New York. The 50th Anniversary of the United Nations was celebrated in part by the members of First Lady Eleanor Roosevelt's family finding and donating items from her real office, and set it up in the United Nations Headquarters in New York.

Eleanor Roosevelt wanted to see the entire world have the Rights Americans were supposed to enjoy, and to learn the Responsibilities of each human on earth to make sure humans could build a lasting peace on earth Without the United States becoming just another land grubbing, genocidal empire builder in the long history of such governments in the world, to instead retain and build on the vision of the Founders of the United States and the writers of the United States Constitution, which they hoped had formed a new form of governance, a government OF the PEOPLE, BY the PEOPLE, and FOR the PEOPLE that would by the eternal vigilance and participation of ALL on American soils to be capable of constant contemplation and rebuilding of a BETTER regulation OF the PEOPLE, BY the PEOPLE, FOR the PEOPLE.

Eleanor wanted, in her push to facilitate the founding of the United Nations to let other nations, and other people around the globe learn about American PEOPLE based governance, and to teach ALL people on the earth that to have RIGHTS, everyone must accept RESPONSIBILITIES to keep the dream from faltering.

To teach your family about the Constitution, it is necessary to know about the earth itself. These facts are taught in many pre-schools and kindergartens because in order for the children to be tested and accepted into the most prestigious of private schools, the children will have to pass testing with these facts on them in January of their Kindergarten year, at the average age of five and six months.

There are web sites, museum sites, and many educational book and kit sites that either provide free education in these areas, or provide kits and workbooks to help your family learn these facts every human needs to know.

The Universe.

The Universe is the cradle of the earth. The easiest way to teach this concept is to buy workbooks for young children and work with children in your family to learn these concepts.

Religion. ALL religions have their own view of how the universe was formed and how the earth and other parts of the universe were formed. This book is NOT going to argue any one theory. The theory as presented, a huge space, with billions of planets, solar systems, and our own solar system with our one earth and the continents of today, and how they are divided up by oceans is more than enough information for a five year old to learn to help that young person understand we ALL have to have responsibilities in order to enjoy rights in human society. It is up to each parent and each person in America to learn and know the theories and make up their own mind, while respecting the right of others to have a different view point. One of the most important viewpoints of America is that we ALL have a right to our own belief, in finance, education, in religion, in relationships, in science, as long as we do NOT harm others.

Most educational and scientific bookstores and websites sell simple cardboard, to extremely complex and expensive models of the solar system and the earth.

A globe and world map are both great gifts to the family to learn about the earth, and to set goals for seeing and learning about the world.

There are several inexpensive puzzles, to a few expensive wooden puzzles of the United States of America and the territories included in the Rights of the Constitution and necessarily the Responsibilities each person on any American soil needs to learn and take to heart.

For those who have children in the earliest Cub Scouts, or Brownies, Pathfinders, or Camp Fire programs there usually are badges, awards, and suggested learning programs for learning the set up of our solar system and the continents and countries of the earth we live on.

Nations. States, Counties, City, Street, Address, A five year old NEEDS to know the answer to each of these questions. They need to have a map of their own state, and their own county, and city to know where they live and how to find that exact pinpoint on a world map, and globe.

# HISTORY

Children need to understand that history, like religion, is in the eye and belief of the beholder.

Native Americans, and Natives of other lands have a far different version of history than that of the empire builders, who in the late 1400's developed guns, canons and genocide in order to take what belonged to others. A massive difference in the breaching of the treaties given by George Washington that NOT ONE MORE acre, nor one more Native life would be taken due to the Natives helping his troops win the Revolutionary War and other wars up to current wars. The Native Americans are the highest ratio of Americans to military personnel of any race in the Americas. Yet Native Americans still live in areas without running water, electricity, or phone service, let alone cell phone or cable service. To be fair, while watching the CSPAN covered hearing of the FCC about rural area cell service bills, there are even Congresspersons, Senators, Governors and other leadership in rural states that discussed their own need to stand on the couch, wave the phone, and miss most of the big games unless they went to a big town and rented a hotel room with wi-fi and satellite sports cable.

Children at five are old enough to understand that taking things by force is not OK.

Children at five are old enough to understand that a few Founders convinced others they were tired of working hard, and having what they worked for taken by gunpoint to pay for the rich lifestyle of people thousands of miles away who had decided they deserved something that was not theirs. That used force, and greed to get others to go and take guns and canons and take lands and assets from others.

Children at five are old enough to understand the concepts of the Constitution. That ALL people are created equal, and have equal rights to life, liberty and the pursuit of happiness.

Note: in on site work in lock downs and probation programs it was found few, if any, of the criminal juveniles or adults had a concept of self worth, let alone the worth of others. It is necessary to train all people on American soils to value life, liberty and the right to pursue happiness. Happiness is NOT what I want, and a five year old can and does understand readily the concept of the difference between want, need, and MINE and YOURS.

Recent news events have shown that it is important that ALL people on American (and global) soil NEED to have a concept of MINE and YOURS. More than 11,000 people are out of their homes, evacuated in one area of S. California because a young man through family, school, society, was not responsibly taught the concepts of MINE, YOURS, and anger management and due to a fight with a neighbor set one of the most deadly and land consuming forest fires in California history.

Another young man is being arraigned for murder, but he is hiding in his cell, shouting for his doctor. This is a reality for many school districts being paid for "special ed" students that are NOT special education, they are in fact behavior disordered students that need to have EFFECTIVE and responsible programs. They NEED to be made aware of the reality that they are NOT "special", but instead disabled and need to able themselves as much as possible and learn to control their behavior.

One day, while teaching "Youth Protection Act" at a school, the teacher had a young volunteer from the community teaching about journal writing. He had brought new journals for each student. One of the students refused to write. I knew him, and he trusted me, so I said to him. This is for you. It will help you and he began to write. He wrote "all the teachers do is yell at the bad kids, and we do not learn anything, and no one cares". I cared. I asked if I could copy the page, and mail it to the President. He said yes, I mailed a copy with a letter to President Bush. He started "No Child Left Behind". His concept was NO CHILD LEFT BEHIND. By the time the money and the idea came through the bureaucracy it was, at least in that district, any student the teachers did not want sent to a "special" classroom at the ed center where they learned NOTHING and beat each other up until they could manage to not come any more. In later probation programs I met some of those youth. Many were in a holding mental health facility until they turned eighteen when they would be put in adult prison for crimes they had committed, others worked hard, and learned and changed their lives before getting to that dead end place. At least one of the special ed teachers who had a great record of retrieving and anchoring special ed kids was fired for refusing to "teach" a new program that made it mandatory to teach a certain lesson, from a certain book, at all times, and the district had hired what the teachers called "the school police" to go peek in doors and enforce this program. HOW can one teach a program to youth who are not even able to read, or do not speak English? This teacher had taken it upon herself, WITH the help of the students at all grade levels to create lesson plans to help them catch UP and get caught up in all areas in that mandated Nazi system of forced "learning". Other teachers, observed while I was teaching Youth Protection Act in more than one District, in many schools and classes, place smarter kids next to those who could NOT do the work so they could cheat and mark the little boxes with enough correct answers to let the teacher keep the job, NOT teach the students anything but to cheat.

WE as a nation need to teach parents how to teach their children to LOVE learning. Not just the nuts and bolts to get a robot technical job, or job doing the bureaucratic support for a system that day by day becomes LESS humane and LESS of the People, by the People and FOR the People as our Constitution says we must. A system that teaches ALL facets of real history and mistakes of humanity, as well as great ideas and inventions by ALL humanity and to enjoy art, music, sports, dance, drama from ALL nations, and backgrounds, as well as our own unique growing and shifting American perspectives in ALL educational backgrounds.

PARENTS, to make sure their children are living "happily ever after" each day in school need to get down to the school and see what is really going on. Parents NEED to read the Constitution and realize that our children are in prisons, where they suffer needlessly daily from gangs, violence, racism, and worst, the lack of care and ability of the school district to make sure the students are learning and more importantly learning to LOVE to learn. At home, teach your child to balance life. READ to your children, let them see you read. Whether on the computer, or in a book read out loud, or listen to recorded books WITH your children and discuss what you all shared. Teach your children that reading is a great and important part of life. Reading is like meeting one or more friends who share with YOU and anyone else who reads or shares in the book content.

TEACH your children and others that movies and television give us a peek in a window, reading the book gives us a peek into the soul of the material and the author. Talk to your own family and friends, if THEY are NOT represented in reading material, help the children and teens to write books after listening to what I call "Grandparent stories".

Give a copy to the person who told you the story, ask them for editing and additional material. SHARE what you have written. Give a final copy to the person who told the story. People often are more concerned with making sure a private detective or the FBI says it ALL is true, true, true. Sometimes how a person experienced life, or the humorous telling of tales from a life are more educational than the exact truth.

Watch and participate in educational television shows WITH your children, if the neighbors ignored children are there, teach them too. ASK their parents to come and participate. Let them see YOU watch a gardening show, and plant a garden, learn and enjoy group sewing, art, or cooking shows, or find home repair, art, gardening, sewing, cooking shows and show the children and teens. Let them see YOU have the courage to find out HOW to do things, and risk doing them wrong until you get it right.

There are programs in other countries, and expensive private programs that teach these concepts, but the overall review of "special ed" programs reveals the school districts taking the extra money, but not providing the proper and appropriate support and encouragement for "special" students. All of these issues need to be addressed for us to be able to "LIVE" happily ever after. Keep in mind at all times one can find a place to resolve part of these issues, while maintaining their own ability to live "happily ever after".

# DRUGS, CRIME, SUICIDE, MENTAL HEALTH CARE

These are important issues for Americans to resolve. Drugs often cause criminal activity; as well as create worse criminal behavior by drug addicted mentally ill persons, and suicidal persons.

WE as a nation need to stop pretending there are ANY perfect persons. There are just those who hide their flaws better and those who either can not, or do not hide their flaws and less socially acceptable behaviors. I LOVED it when Tuesday night in the election speeches O'Rourke, candidate for Senate thanked his supporters and volunteers, even though the run had been unsuccessful, and said they were the best fucking supporters. I loved it when President Bush, while President, forgot his mike was live and said "I hate that asshole". I would rather people be real, than stress themselves out to pretend to be what whoever it is thinks a person has to be to be perfect.

We as a nation NEED to stop playing Cops and Robbers with the mentally ill, the socially irresponsible, AND the drug addicted. We as a nation NEED to find resolution to the problems and make sure even the youngest of children are supported in getting help needed and dealing with the horrors and realities of life in a positive, rather than negative way. Las Vegas police decided if there was nowhere to refer the mentally ill, and/or homeless, they would make it an operation of the police department. IF a person needs help, they are put in a place to get help. The project is not in operation long enough to have firm statistics, but at the very least, homeless and mentally ill persons are beginning to know that they do NOT get to go to Las Vegas and just wander around anymore.

DRUGS are represented in movies, television shows, and music videos as being "wink, wink" good things the authorities do not want us to enjoy. That is NOT true. If a person NEEDS drugs, they need to know, early on, that they need to see a doctor, a psychiatrist and therapists to keep their antisocial antics in control. They are NOT trendy people. Others are too afraid to live their lives without drugs, or have gotten addicted to prescription medications and are afraid to seek help.

People take drugs because they are incapable of dealing with life and instead of seeking professional help, they hang out with other "trendy" people and cause more sadness, horror, and crime in the world.

We NEED to teach our children to deal with life. We NEED to teach drug addicts to identify how they started to take drugs, and how it led them to crime and harming other people and that it is NOT trendy and fashionable.

There was a story today (September 25,2018) on a Yahoo Email opening site, it was about a teacher who realized she had learned from a student how to be a teacher. The story is about a student she read in the past year assessments had been a great student, then turned into a monster child. She "taught" him, sternly, firmly, he failed, she admitted she enjoyed red marking his papers, and giving him F grades. THEN she read his file. She found that when his Mother had died of cancer, his life had changed. His father had gone into deep depression, leaving the child with no one. She began to change HER attitude and ways, and he began to heal and get motivated. He wrote her letters over the years, always thanking her. When he graduated from Medical School, he told her he had set a goal to help others as she had helped him. He got married, he asked her to sit in the Groom's Mother's chair since his Father had also passed away and he had no family. This story needs to inspire all who interact or work with other humans.

# 48 ACRES Projects

This is the background of the 48 Acre proposal submitted in response to a request from Community Redevelopment to create a fast, efficient and effective veteran support program for an estimated 70,000 veterans being expected to return in one two year period from the Afghanistan/Iraq wars. The project was based on a three tiered system for women with children who had survived Domestic Violence some years earlier. That project was built and implemented in Los Angeles, but the Developer had created a problem that allowed him to purchase the project and land in a closed non-announced bid sale. It taught us to create a new paragraph and signature required agreement for every board member, staff member and volunteer in any of our programs to protect the assets for use by the intended persons.

## *"48 Acres"*

Three Tiered Treatment and Housing Systems

EXECUTIVE SUMMARY

Three tiered Treatment and Housing Systems are designed for local community use to resolve the issues of citizens that need a hand up, and for most, to work their way into mainstream society without the problems and issues that often cause them to become criminals, or upgrade criminal and violent behavior.

Utilizing local resources, land use, tax reduction, volunteers, the cost of the systems is reduced and the residents are able to afford the tier they need. The police, medical and mental health community have resources locally to positively address issues and problems.

These systems address the issues of veterans, homeless, and others being forced into programs in substandard areas rather than being in the mainstream of the local area. These systems address the issues of treatment programs being so cramped and over populated they become depressing in themselves to those needing the services.

# BACKGROUND

Developed by Miriam Negri, Founder and Owner of IDESIGN ARCHITECTURE and a Los Angeles Redevelopment Specialist with professionals and volunteers to address the needs and issues of survivors of Domestic Violence and their families, the first three tiered system was put in place for single mother survivors of Domestic Violence for Court Mandated families.

The model was then used to develop a proposal when requested by Redevelopment to address the needs and problems of young veterans returning to one area of the city where 70,000 veterans were expected over the ensuing two years to return to that one area. Utilizing a 48 acre abandoned military barracks site, on 48 Acres, the team of volunteers developed a proposal to house an interactive program for those veterans and their families as the veterans returned home.

Some of the group of volunteers had been asked following Desert Storm to create an equine therapeutic program for women veterans who had been court mandated due to problems with violence from PTSD that made their homes unsafe for their children.

At one point, one of the volunteers, who was a Credentialed Special Education teacher and had designed programs for the White Mountain Apache Nation, as well as many rural and ghetto area school districts for high risk youth and their families was injured at work and began to volunteer her expertise and advice to the program development for the 48 Acres.

One of the Founders of a Homes for Heroes, a small project run locally for PTSD veterans in remodeled homes for six to ten veterans with similar issues was asked to bring a member to Washington DC for a meeting of Congresspersons on the problems of the returning veterans and their families.

Patricia McClaughlin at her own expense paid for herself and several of the women veteran project and Homes for Heroes Directors to travel to Washington DC to testify in this hearing. One young veteran testified that due to having been raped during active duty in country where combat was occurring she had come home and resigned from the military at the end of her enlistment. She had suffered nightmares, and stress which was labeled PTSD. She said her one dream was to be capable of living with her children, and to have them run in and jump on the bed, laugh and read comics together, and go make pancakes shaped like animals. But, due to the fact that if she heard the slightest sound in the night and was up and holding one of her children to the wall in a combat defense hold, her children were court mandated to not be allowed to spend a night with her. The only way she could see her children was in a protected program overseen by a Court appointed liaison official.

Patricia brought this problem home, and the equine therapy project designed day "camping Sundays" which allowed the mothers in these Court mandated programs to attend classes and become safe enough to attend an afternoon program in which they brought tents and their court liaisons and created the bed out of sleeping bags and blankets in the big horse arena to have the romp on the bed, read books and comics, and then have a big community pancake breakfast in which the mothers could make pancakes shaped like animals with their children and the liaisons.

Working with psychologists and therapists from the VA and local Court liaison programs educational programs were designed to help the veterans realize they were dangerous to their children, and the issue was not to "get" their children back, but instead to heal to a place where they themselves were confident the children would be safe with them. Utilizing the women themselves to develop these programs they were highly successful.

A California Congressperson said she wanted to begin to fund and build these programs, that the therapeutic programs, which had existed as a disabled special Crew of the Boy

Scouts of America, needed to get their own 501 3 c filing and bank accounts. This was done. IRS promised a special agent to assist in the charitable filing and program support to keep the pilot and on going builds legal and within IRS guidelines.

The formal proposal was developed.

While the members of the Board were filling out the paperwork for the By Laws, and IRS filings, Patricia was in the restroom when the line marked "DIRECTOR" came up, In line with military philosophy, she was not there to step back fast enough to not end up being the Director. Complying with IRS directives and experience with other charitable projects, the Board decided to have email rather than in person meetings, with one annual meeting to read the ongoing minutes and financial reports. A bank account was established, an accountant volunteered his services until the program was making enough money that the work created a demand that he be paid for annual reports, One member was assigned to keep records. The Director and two others were assigned to sign ALL checks or withdrawals of over $1000 as directed by the by laws. TWO signatures were required for all other checks, and the decision was made to not use ATM due to risk of funds being hacked or embezzled.

The members discussed and adopted a provision that at any time a member, or employee attempted to take funds, or assets, to put in place a simple, yet binding procedure to send them a "we understand people have other obligations, and we thank you for your service" card, the same card sent to all volunteers and staff that resigned for personal reasons, to avoid law suits, This was based on the reality that a developer on the initial Domestic Violence project, even with the oversight of City Counsel, and Council had managed to get control of the property after it was developed, and at a closed auction purchase the entire real estate and buildings for pennies on the dollars.

This was tested twice. One person receiving a card went to a lawyer, who told her that just by coming to him, she had breached her statement that she understood and accepted this clause before joining the project. Unfortunately even volunteers and clients have had to sign this agreement, due to theft of equipment, and even animals from the program.

Many parts of tier one are day activities and programs. Upon contacting local VFW, American Legions, and VA facilities as well as other volunteer and veteran run programs it was well supported that many veterans and their families could benefit from day programs while living at home. This allowed the question of the VA to supply their own therapists, physical therapists and clinicians to the 48 Acre sites. Due to the large number of veterans and family members treated, the buildings, and sites, such as gyms, special pools, and spas and meeting rooms and outdoor meeting areas as well as Equitherapy© and Aquatherapy© programs the VA could avoid the problems of veterans getting to the VA and also the costs of transport, parking and support staff. The programs were designed to utilize veterans, trained and in education programs to become the professionals needed rather than need so much paid and VA fund draining programs.

Utilizing volunteers also gave community members an opportunity to learn more about the real life issues of returning veterans and their families. Local veteran program social workers, with overwhelming caseloads often referred veterans or their families to our programs for help in problems the VA was not addressing, or did not have programs building to address.

On the operating sites for day use seniors and disabled persons as well as professional graduate students who needed interning hours were a great opportunity for both the volunteers, and the veterans and family members.

We have written a book, an inclusion book about all of the programs to help high risk youth and veteran family members and veterans who are not able to attend real ranch experience. Carousel Horse is a novel, and contains a screenplay which we expect to produce about the programs and how they work. Two new books will be published soon about veterans and their families, and about women veterans in their own programs.

The decision to divide programs was made early in the programs as the needs of each veteran and family member vary. Each person learns about the programs and is free to select the programs either they, or their therapists and psychiatrists deem most helpful for their issues.

48 Acres was blessed with psychiatrists of high stature and private practice who donated time and expertise to designing the programs. Some of the therapists were past medics from in country combat medic work. One of the programs is named "DR PETE" for the medic, psychologist that taught us so much, and has left as his legacy the love of the veterans, and the responsibility to listen to THEM, not use our super hero healing powers to MAKE them better.

Being open to learning at all times is the responsibility of all staff and volunteers, and as they grow in the programs the veterans and family members themselves.

There are many other programs and learning from the best of them, as well as those who use horses as couches rather than let the animals do their innate healing is something we attempt to teach others. Programs based on a NEED for severely physically disabled children and youth are NOT the appropriate programs for combat crushed soldiers and their family members.

**"Soldiers are not like other people".… Anonymous combat survivor**

"Each of these veterans, once was physically, emotionally, mentally found fit enough to put their life on the line for this country, you WILL treat them with the respect and care they have earned and deserve. IF they have become injured, or emotionally, or mentally unsound, it was living through things the rest of us could never imagine, let alone live through" Lt. Melendez, Doctor at the Sepulveda VA Hospital Critical Mental Ward, 1978.

Whether Army, Navy, Marines, Air Force, or Special Ops of any of these services, soldiers have lived something the rest of us will not EVER live through.

Treat soldiers as professional humans and they will come back to themselves and teach each other to be their own best selves. This was the advice of an old VFW leader, and also the advice of the Founder and Director of VEA which is the educational program we utilize for our veterans (now open to other groups, such as single mothers, and aging out foster kids).

One of our PhD, MD doctors taught us that if we know we are OK and treat others as if they are OK, it may take time, but they will rise to the top.

One of the PhD. Domestic Violence instructors and Founders of a successful DV program which is taught in many colleges and universities taught us that people like to succeed and will rise to their own top level, IF we do not treat them as less, or those we can "heal". Many times soldiers heal each other. The animals heal fast and by instinct. We therefore decided to NOT use our horses as couches, and while there are

AquaTherapy© and EquiTherapy© programs, they are NOT psycho-social treatment, they are animal healing realities.

Our programs are designed to be FREE, and to be as ongoing as the person needs and wants, some of our volunteers have been program members long ago. We call everyone "riders" as we "enjoy the ride" of life, or learn to enjoy it once again.

We decided early on we would rather have someone who is not a veteran come and learn to heal, than to waste money on bureaucratic "qualification" paperwork. Each of our sessions, IF recommended by a therapist, or psychiatrist is written up on one page by the staff class director of the day, it is sent to the treating therapist, by email only, as modeled by many group treatment facilities for the State itself, and kept only by numbered reference for ONE WEEK and discarded.

This is only done with the signed agreement of the rider.

Some areas, such as the sweat lodges, Passing stick groups, or Twelve Step groups are between the members of the group. While a staff member is present, they are not allowed to write down and report to therapists or the VA unless discussed, and the writing signed by the rider.

One place we have had all our riders acknowledge is child abuse. When these problems arise, they are reported both to the police and the treating VA or therapists and psychiatrists, not in a punitive manner, but to protect the children. Having created this huge block to honesty, we created programs WITH juvenile judges and therapists to treat the entire family for healing, NOT punitive goals.

The reality is that many veterans have serious issues with violence. They are trained killers not in control of themselves, and NEED a safe place to work on these issues, there are several programs across the country created and run by veterans themselves that acknowledge these issues and help veterans deal with them. These programs are currently in proposal to the VA and Department of Defense, as well as to the Department of Justice as Veteran Legal programs to facilitate debriefing of a combat ready mind, and helping veterans (and active duty) service members be able to freely address their issues and admit to them BEFORE they harm others, often their own family members or community members. Child and spousal abuse is often included in this form of PTSD.

The newest studies at the VA itself are showing that concussion injuries to the brain often create a loss of ability to control impulse as well as many other forms of PTSD misdiagnosis. We urge our veterans to ask for an exploration by the VA of newly discovered neurological injuries that result in problems NOT PTSD. They are brain and neurological injuries, NOT mental or emotional responses to war. The injury to the neuro parts of the brain and neurological systems that control appropriate behavior and inhibitions of acting out of anger and other negative emotions need careful handling and training for the newly identified issues for these trained killers.

This was based on the open treatment programs for high risk youth designed into many of our programs for high risk youth in probation and foster group home care, as well as based on the Youth Protection Act, which we taught for several years FREE in schools. The Act seems to have disappeared, along with the mandatory training program that ALL teachers and principals were supposed to teach, but the Union, goaded by teachers who hated the program appear to have "won". This program taught children and youth what they need to be protected FROM, and how to get help, if not from a teacher, from the Principal, or a police officer or fireperson, or at an emergency room, and to go and report so injuries could be documented.

Each site is expected to have animal assisted programs. The goal is to allow the animals to heal rather than to use them as couches or appendages of a psychiatric modality. Many residents have or will acquire companion animals, each tier is mandated to allow animals, and to provide supportive training and care for the animals as required by each resident.

The drawing is for 48 acres or more. (this is not included in the book, only the proposal packages, but can be requested for groups wanting to build a complex community treatment first step site.

The scale is left out to show the idea, rather than the exact site.

Each site, of course, due to local code enforcement, permits, building codes, etc and location, will have to be unique and done exactly when the land is acquired.

Each site will be created for its exact purpose.

These purposes have included Domestic Violence Survivors programs, Senior housing, Disabled housing, Independent Mental Illness treatment and independent living projects, veteran and veteran family programs, refugee relocation and city redevelopment programs.

BEFORE land is acquired inquiries need to be made to get the support of the local city council and preliminary thoughts from the building and zoning departments as to how hard it will be to create reality on that exact piece of land before beginning to estimate costs and break the project down into doable units.

IF you have military base, VA or HUD property it is much easier to deal with, as the agencies deal with the land acquirement and use politics.

The 48 acre and more sites will ALL have level one and two apartments, townhouses and condos. In each area the local developers will be contacted for support on tier three new housing, especially for veterans needing physical disability modifications in the housing prior to the designs being submitted to building and zoning. If redeveloping an area, both investors and developers will be approached for building the complete three tiered systems. There is one private gated community in Rialto, California, developed by a commercial developer, that is sold and operational as an expensive and protected citizen housing program which has most of the features needed for a Three Tiered Treatment or Housing System, this proves the real estate development is feasible to support proposals to government agencies, as well as banks and private investors, or funders through the National Homes for Heroes Development charitable Foundation 501 3 c tax filing programs.

Each facility is expected to have its own local Board, related to the creative need, and its own LLC in the state where it is located, but will be listed through National Homes for Heroes Master Oversight Board to reduce Administrative costs as well as risk of loss of property or funding in any manner.

One bank account, with ONE trust account to be managed and overseen by each Board, the National Board, and the facilitating Accountant and Legal team will keep the finances transparent on a daily basis to IRS, the State, and all government agencies and private funders. The bylaws provide a quick, humane way of dealing with these situations. This system has been tested, the person involved went to a law firm that told them, just by coming here you have breached the agreements and given up any right to dispute this finding. This was inserted after loss experiences with developers, grant programs and even volunteers in the programs.

# THE SITE DEVELOPMENT

Private parking will be available for all units, handicapped parking will be designated throughout the acreage as well. Near the arenas, physical therapy, water therapy and gardens as well as the equine therapy barns and/or round corrals will be parking for busses and vans as necessary. Vans and busses will be scheduled as much as possible on pick up/drop off of one group after another to minimize the number of empty vehicles parked at any one time.

The sites will have shuttle service on the lap road. Disabled person transport will be available as well.

The goal is to have flex solar energy systems on all parking structures and roofed areas to accomplish with wind resources a negative power use for the complexes. Several research projects and private companies have been approached on this goal and say it is possible and easily accomplished. Some major electric suppliers, including municipal and private energy companies have been approached and say this is easily accomplished, and they are already approved for training and working with veterans.

It is suggested that first time offenders in low income areas be given the opportunity to train and hired for this type of job in restructuring rural and urban low cost housing areas. Both Probation and Parole have been approached on this approach to innovative probation and parole programs and have said, yes, let us know as it begins. The Veteran Courts, and Veteran Legal programs have all said YES to this as a proposed rehabilitation and career training program for which they are already funded.

If a 48 Acre site is designed to treat and house low level, non violent offenders, the system is easily reworked. This same project can be reworked for foster children who are aging out of the system with nowhere to go,. Special programming and support programs are designed for foster youth, both to help themselves, and to provide inspiration and support for children and youth coming up behind them in the foster court systems.

The forty eight and larger acreage sites will have recruited training facilities from chain stores and restaurants to serve the tenants on the site, to serve outside patrons during regular store hours, and to train veterans for jobs when they leave the tier one and tier two living sites. NHH/SH2 is active in recruiting service companies and installation companies for disabled housing as appropriate for large nearby developments and cities with veteran disabled populations that will create work installing and maintaining special equipment in third tier housing.

The gardens are the Horicultural Therapy portion of each of the sites. Flowers, fruits, vegetables are all included in the therapeutic gardens. The sites with apartments and townhouses ALL have small growing areas, the residents are expected to grow something, even if just lawn, or potted plants that they can use for their therapeutic time at home.

Some of the major fencing surrounding the pools, gardens, arenas, and outer security walls and fencing will have fruits, honeysuckle, vegetables, grapes and flowers growing so the residents and therapy members can feel free to help keep them up, and to eat the fruits, vegetables, berries and grapes. Each site will be expected to work in community fund raising events to sell crafts, fruit and vegetables. ALL tenants and day clients who come into the programs for day only will work in the occupational, Hortitherapy©, equine, K-9, and other Animalassistedtherapy© and Equtherapy© and Aquatherapy© programs as well as choose among the art, drama, and craft programs which support group therapy programs.

Every site will have gray water retrieval to service the garden areas. The City of Pasadena has piloted and is modeling programs for this type of water retrieval. Cal Tech, among other Technology programs now have students doing research on using retrieved water from storms in many ways, both to reduce damage to the streets and sewers from major influx of storm water, and to increase available water resources in many areas.

The Chairs of these programs have expressed interest in any site being used as a class project for their current students to design, build and implement the use of research programs, for which they are expected to raise their own funding as part of their degree requirements. Since the time these programs were designed, new water programs have been invented and are piloting from many technical colleges and universities. These programs include pollution used as a system for water retrieval, and fog used as water retrieval as well as use of all building run off for water retrieval.

The fire departments have expressed interest in developing the pools and therapy pools developed for use as fire suppression resources for the helicopters, and also fire suppression ponds which can be used for fishing and local nature while supplying local resources for the fire departments, state and federal use in water dumping helicopter use. These are often used to reduce property tax, and therefore rent on the properties, reducing the cost to each tenant for their treatment and second tier housing.

All of the sites will have as much solar as possible. We expect to show case the newest forms of solar water heating and other energy concepts by asking the companies to showcase their products and give discounts for any of the third tier homes that can afford them.

Wind energy is also being researched, the fans are becoming smaller and much more effective at saving energy and transmitting it to local energy companies for use and storage. In all areas where a site is created wind energy use will be researched as well to reduce the costs to the residents, and give as many residents as possible an opportunity for jobs in these newly developing fields. Veterans we have found, are often funded for this type of work program through special veteran programs.

Green energy is part of the architecture, and it is part of the therapy. As the level two goal is to facilitate jobs for veterans and their family members, green energy is a growing field. Veterans are encouraged to go to school to be cutting edge developers, and installers and maintainers of green energy sources for urban, suburban and rural areas. (when these sites are used for disabled, or senior, or low income residence three tier and first time home owner programs the on site job work, and inspiration for an education to work part time on their own site will be an additional positive goal for green programs.

The forty eight acre and bigger sites will be recruiting private dental programs (or Native American dental programs for Native American veteran based sites) and recruiting veterans and their family members to maintain long hour dental clinics in storefronts on the site to be rented out for that purpose. In areas where the VA will provide the dentists and equipment, the site will provide the dental clinic space and/or mobile dental clinics for the members of the site project.

A "main street" design will be incorporated with real businesses using the store fronts provided to give training to the residents in jobs before they are moved to a higher tier and into "real" jobs out in the community. Security at all facilities will be gated, fenced communities to reduce opposition of the building of each site in a local area, and also to protect the public from the residents as needed. There are many programs on rural and wilderness backed ranches and farms that specialize in the treatment and restoration of violent residents. Veterans in particular need what they need, small, self sustained units have been created on these ranches to provide the most healing environment possible for the veterans. One special ops Marine for over 25 years spent the next 25 years of his life out on the range with his horses wrangling cattle and horses for large ranch complexes. He went back to school, became a veterinarian, and found his job was putting down horses misused by their owners, and had what today is called a PTSD break and went to work on the ranch.

Several veterans are in documentaries who have gone into a room and stayed for years, often only coming out for trips to the doctor, and one day, for whatever their reason, coming out, going back to work or school and veteran support programs. The small self sustained housing on ranches and game preserves give those not readily able to have family or support to live alone long enough to heal a connection with reality, as well as time to heal in a calm, and quiet program where both therapy and some regulation helps them to heal.

10 and less acreage sites concept drawing: Not included in this book

This drawing is a concept for 10 or less acres. Even a one acre site can contain ONE level two house for the site supervising couple (at least one must be a vet, or active duty military) to live on the site, the day and evening clinics and therapy programs give a site such as this a large capacity for the number of veterans and their families that can be treated at such a small facility.

The therapy buildings and modules will be added as the local zoning and building permits allow, and the land supports.

The ideal goal is to have local VA facilities send day program persons out to the sites in vans and by bus. These will go back and pick up other day members, and shuttle back and forth to the VA and base facilities to decrease parking needs, and annoyance to the local community from too much traffic.

Because veterans and active duty families are working, and in school, the programs are expected to start early in the day and extend late into the night, in order to promote maximum use of the program buildings and assets. Each site is expected to have one 24/7 clinic with at least a triaging Physician, Assistant that can utilize the onsite ambulance service to take veterans to the nearest VA Emergency Admission Center when needed. The Veterans Administration was approached and very eager to develop systems that would reduce the need for their own facilities to have a backlog of cases due to an ongoing and more personal VA provided system depending on the size and population of the site.

Non veteran sites would have a similar program with local emergency hospitals and ambulance services to provide the fastest most efficient treatment possible, while reducing costs to the local community for non emergent problems as well as other resources for the tenants to best address their needs in a positive and efficient system.

The ideal is for the VA to provide therapeutic support if we provide the rooms for therapy, the gyms for physical therapy, and the pools, and other therapeutic areas. This will allow Healthwalk to provide therapists and oversee the VA staff needs, and NHH/SH2 to only have to deal with independent living quarters. (Townhouses and condo's on site-and facilitating home ownership, or long term lease of homes off site for tier three). Which reduces the need for additional permits, state licensing, etc.

**Suggested uses for Three Tiered Programs:**

Domestic Violence Survivors programs
Senior housing
Disabled housing
Independent Mental Illness treatment and independent living projects
Homeless re-entry programs

Veteran and veteran family program
Migrant Labor Housing and Education programs
Refugee relocation and city redevelopment programs.

## Domestic Violence Survivors programs

The original three tiered project was designed by Miriam Negri, along with Los Angeles Redevelopment Agency to provide tiered housing for Survivors of Domestic Violence and their Children.

First tier in this program was designed for the children to be safe, and have 24/7 supervision and care, with special education programs to facilitate the Court Mandated programs removing children from homes where they were endangered due to Domestic Violence in the homes. The second tier was designated condo, or apartment living within local areas to the families becoming independent and in third tier either renting or purchasing permanent housing, and building a career for the single parent as needed.

Research had shown that two years in group therapy is the norm for women to address their issues and not continue their violent relationships. These programs were designed to protect both the women and children from violent relationships and displays. The program was based on more than twenty years of programs developed by volunteers and staff psychologists to facilitate healing for Court mandated women into DV programs.

## Senior housing

Senior housing was designed for seniors either owning, or renting their own homes. This project was designed for seniors to be part of a tier one community self help program and if needed to move into tier two supported living as needed. Tier one itself was designed to have hospice housing in rented apartments, or owned/rented housing as needed for each member of the community. ALL units of the three tiers were to be protected by daily health and safety checks, provision of transportation for doctors and shopping in groups as needed.

A community center in the tier one complex was designed for meetings, family celebrations or community celebrations and supportive health and financial classes for members of the community.

This design was based on an existing expensive private gated community. The Developer was prepared to create a modified development for seniors. All senior needs for walk in bath ttubs, cranes for bathing, modified kitchen and cooking areas for wheel chairs were included in the price if designed prior to framing of the units.

## Disabled housing

Disabled housing was designed for specific disabilities. Based on gated complexes designed for disabled and aging veterans, the disabled housing was designed to create gated communities with a central base of medical unit, dental care, and mental health programs for those with specific disabilities. The 24/7 community social work support unit would be to create maximum independent, yet protected and assisted living for the disabled.

All units needing special equipment and design, such as wider doorways, and cranes for bed to bath, or walk in bathtubs, and safe showers for disabled persons were discussed with developers and contractors. As long as the special designs were approved prior to framing, the developers and contractors agreed to putting them in without extra cost. If older housing had to be remodeled the cost can be extreme due to code enforcement and permit fees, and requirements to reframe parts of the home or apartment.

Independent Mental Illness treatment, drug and alcohol, and independent living projects for tenants as required by psychological need Homeless re-entry programs

A three tiered system for homeless re-entry programs is designed for tier one to concentrate evaluations of health, mental ability and disability as well as drug, alcohol, or other criminal and/or issues. The second tier of any of these programs may be entered as soon as 24 hour evaluations are complete, if the tenant is not referred to an appropriate first tier for alcohol, drugs, or other addiction, or mental illness programs. Those with financial and work problems are in a separate program with a fast tracked program to help the tenants move forward, while dealing with the realities of why they became homeless, and re-enter mainstream life as soon as possible.

Often the homeless are veterans and they will be referred within hours to the appropriate veteran tier one program.

## Veteran and veteran family program

It was observed that the high risk youth in many programs had veterans as parents, grandparents, and PTSD had been a significant impacting force on the entire family.

Veterans and their families are referred immediately to first tier programs with at least six day programs for emergencies, and 24/7 contact support lines to facilitate their getting to the program at the earliest time and date possible for evaluation and orientation to the programs.

## Migrant Labor Housing and Education programs

The three tiered housing program was designed for another country to help them facilitate large numbers of labor forces that are migratory and temporary. The tiered housing programs facilitate for the migrant labor workers (and families if they are in the country as well) to stabilize, set goals, and get education, health and other needed help to work towards tier two goals for their return to their home countries. In some nations the matching fund program designed in the initial program worked to encourage the workers to begin to gain skills, take free programs to learn about finance, business management and take their matching funds from the host work country back home to begin to build their own skills and forward the information and skills to others.

Tier three in this program was designed to work with the countries the workers come from to facilitate the design and implementation of small communities, including farm communities, or free roaming herd communities of tradition of those workers to help them rebuild and reenter their own lives, often torn apart by war, famine, or other natural disasters.

## Refugee relocation and city redevelopment programs

Like Migrant Labor Housing programs refugee relocation programs work to rapidly identify needs, assets, and leadership in the refugee communities. This project was inspired by several refugee programs and the real programs that occur in countries with war forcing the people into refugee situations, or to live without water, energy, and/or food supplies for lengthy periods of time.

The inspirational stories of women who have lost their husbands, brothers and sons, yet one day after a major bombing find a partially bombed out school, or apartment building and set up an ad hoc child, elder and disabled program in which the children are in class and back on their educational track one day after a bombing created the ideas and research into the need and reality of people who are addressing these problems.

One Afghanistan refugee camp and a Syrian refugee camp, as well as a mixed refugee camp in Kenya have shown the women marking out little home plots for a "house" whether built from blankets salvaged and brought with them, or United Nations tents, or just garbage they salvage to build shelters for the children and elders and disabled. These women have marked our streets, and school areas. Some have been fortunate to have religious groups, or United Nations programs dig wells and have water that is clean to gather in pots, or bottles as they have salvaged. They have designed sanitation systems out of what little they can salvage and make sure everyone takes sewage to trenches which are dug, and then covered over as needed to make sure the conditions are sanitary as possible.

There are ideas for many ways to create land base and permanent settlements built on the courage and hard work of these surviving refugees and their families.

Tier One would be to utilize the peer identification process, to help educate and supply those so they can rapidly move to tier two, in which housing is supported, and possibly crews can be trained and supplied with machines and needs to establish water, sewage pipes and sewage treatment centers, recycling and garbage centers, and to begin to attract and design work areas to supply needs, and to build local schools.

Tier three would be to move into a more stable property ownership and citizenship for the small settlements to become self sustaining. Many of these refugees are land based. Whether urban or rural, their homes had small farms, and they grew fruit, vegetables and raised small farm animals and often in some areas had small ponds in each home for fresh fish and crayfish based on a program piloted since reconstruction of Vietnam, Laos and Cambodia by private charitable groups. Many of those programs are now established businesses that keep people fed and employed, and the research designers have been successful in putting in solar and wind powered packing and freezing plants. Training programs to keep the packed food clean and sanitary have been very successful. The training in putting in sewage and garbage systems have reduced or eliminated the health problems from using the fish and rice or irrigation ponds from being breeding grounds for disease to be passed on in the sale or barter of the items.

The suggestion is for each community to assess their own need, and begin a community powered proposal. The use of Habitat for Humanity resources, as well as both veteran and reserve volunteer groups, and college volunteer groups helps reduce the costs of building any aspect of any of the programs.

The design for each unit was after many months of research into one and two bedroom suites at exclusive hotels. We believe that our veterans, and those who need a helping hand should be first class, not in skid row areas because the loving citizens do not want "them" in their neighborhood. In at least five recent protests, the protestors themselves are either first generation Americans, or the children of illegal immigrants who themselves were unwanted, but were given a chance by the community they now want to close off to our veterans, and citizens who need help to get on their feet.

One of the most sad stories was in a PBS documentary on veterans which showed a veteran with severe PTSD who was in a treatment facility. It was in skidrow, made out of an ugly old sort of remodeled sweat shop in the old garment district. He went home for the holidays, his parents would not let him in, they thought he lived in a flop house and did not want him around the family children or their friends. He lived in a small room with bunk beds for the several occupants, and they had to eat meals in a slop house type cafeteria. The food was generally from food banks, and low quality. Several of the cooking students at two big colleges had offered to come and cook great meals and teach the veterans to cook with them. Volunteers had offered to bring in tablecloths, and raise money for table settings to make the room more hospitable. They were told just give money.

While many of our events were in partnership with parks, or community centers, we made it a point to get community groups to volunteer and raise money to make each event special and an expression of our thanks for their service to our suffering veterans of all wars. VFW and American Legions are great places to partner up with in this type of event, if for one day, or ongoing programs. The Salvation Army often will donate items needed for the living areas, and churches and community groups seem to like raising funds and buying special items, like a new towel set, or special personal sheet and pillowcase sets for each veteran. Our programs set a goal of wonderful suites. With volunteers, and the donations of Contractors, and State agencies, as well as the VA we had the cost down to $15,000 for each unit. Less than the rented, and ugly refurbished barracks some of the groups put in. One even put up a lovely sign that said, "Homeless Veterans Housing" out front. I would surely feel that would inspire a feeling of being honored and beloved and helping our veterans heal.

# PROGRAMS

]There are many programs for each site, Every new project has its own programs and new ones develop

All of these programs have been further designed, and are available upon request to local, state and federal programs around the world with assistance to plan for their own local area and needs.

## MY MOTHER'S LINENS (MY GRANDMOTHER'S LINENS)

These programs are teas, and using wonderful linen, tablecloths, and dishes brought in by volunteers and staff to remember our Mothers and Grandmothers, and to give a special type of healing meetings for women veterans, and high risk girls who often have no idea of who their mothers, or ancestry is helps heal and build each woman or girl in positive ways. This project is designed by Dr. Pat from Healthwalk Foundation and was designed by their therapists, and VA therapists for use in veteran programs.

DRAGONSLAYERS is the men veteran's design, for use with first responders and veterans. The name was originated by Lt. Vince Cornish, of Cornish Designs who did some of our initial drawings for us and is a creator and Board member for the Turtle Medicine Lodge Projects. A first responder, who had been a CalFire Lt, was laid off when the State budget cuts were created to balance and reduce debt for the State. He was injured in a Construction job while looking for a new fire position. One day he said, "I used to slay dragons", and we all thought that was a perfect one word to describe the men in this particular program. While women in both combat and first responder careers have similar issues, we all agreed that there is a need for separate support groups, and co- event programs for them to work together towards healing. Most of the men in these programs have accomplished more in one day of active duty military or first response work than most humans will accomplish in a lifetime. These are the people who go in, when everyone else is running out and away.

4WHEELIN4WOMEN is a program we are restarting for women veterans, and first responders, critical care nurses and doctors, women paramedics. This program was designed by women to take their children camping and on big Four Wheel weekends together, utilizing the skills of 4 Wheel Jousting, and driving skill events to help the women regain their own confidence and peace of mind.

LITTLE WINGS was a program that was designed by several of the Homes for Heroes Spirit Horse Board members at the request of the YWCA WINGS program and Courts mandating families into domestic violence programs. This program has been changed to fit the needs of children of women combat medics and nurses who have had their children removed from their homes due to violence and instability on the part of one, or both parents. During Desert Storm, the need was expressed by the mandating family court judges for services for the children. Often BOTH parents were combat veterans with PTSD diagnosed, the military and veterans administration had no programs for the children, and the foster care programs had no programs for the children of these circumstances.

## DRAGONMASTERS

This is our NativeNaturalHorsemanship program for high risk youth. The name is based on the study to find out why the immigrants translated the name for horses incorrectly, and the finding that most Native languages, like Hebrew, are base words, with explanatory words to help a person know what is being written or discussed. The disrespectful and demeaning words "magic dog" as translated to the word "horse" was in error. The word for ANY four legged animal, along with its explanatory word meant a four legged animal which had the amazing qualities of what was wrongly translated as "magic". The word actually to Native people is a word which might be more correctly translated as possibly the "spirit of our Creator", the power, the intelligence, the almost dragonlike breath of smoke on cold mornings, or dark cold nights is hard to translate.

Natives know the real meaning. This exercise for the students helped them realize how easy it is to misunderstand and deman others that we do not understand. Dragonmasters is a program that is somewhat like becoming a horse whisperer, or horse listener, or both. These skills, as acquired help heal humans.

Many parents, and program directors wanted to know why the youth were not riding. They mean like cowboys, whopping, socking and kicking horses for their own pleasure. We explained. This program is the first five hundred hours of NativeNaturalHorsemanship, in which the horses train the humans in many skills, one of which is how to handle fear, another how to be a partner, not a horsey rapist. These are important learned skills for risk at high risk of becoming criminals, or suicide statistics.

## EQUINE THERAPY

Spriti Horse II is from the original Sprit Horse Special Crew of Boy Scouts of America that was developed over several years by Felicia Brown, a Horticultural Therapy specialist, and Elizabeth Wiley, horse trainer and equine therapy leader and trainer. The programs were for high risk foster youth, and youth in probation programs. The writing of the book

Carousel Horse was designed to be an inclusion book for study, for those youth that were able to be in the programs as well as those who could only study in their lock down living residence programs.

Spirit Horse II was expanded for veterans, first responders and their families. Spirit Horse II has an animal assisted component that includes dogs, cats, chickens, bunnies, ducks, that are pets of the volunteers, staff and directors.

Often times animals have been taken care of by the program due to the death, or incapacity of their owners, trained and utilized in the programs, welcoming the owners, or family of owners to come and visit as often as possible, and when possible take the animals home. Our Directors at this time have their own pets, trained as therapy animals, as well as therapy animals or companion animals that needed new homes fostered in their homes.

The horses for equine therapy have never been rescue horses, the program is NOT a rescue project. The riders find an support rescue programs, and when possible buy their own animals which they train and bring back as volunteers to use in the programs. The Directing Trainer brought her own horses into the therapy work, and by giving free feed, and often free board to professional horsepersons, had the use of both the owner and animal. The philosophy behind the means of gaining more animals was to provide the riders with top animals, and top training from active professional riders, as well as to make sure should illness, injury, or death of the Director, the animals would have their own families and owners to take over their care, leaving NO burden on local animal control, and no animals without a home. Spirit Horse II when necessary due to Spinal Cord Cancer of the Director and a disabling vehicle accident from drunks racing put the Training Director out of service were housed at a sanctuary, at a discount, where they are allowed to be utilized in treatment and veteran programs.

## EDUCATION PROGRAMS

Every project in our group has an education component. Dr. David Hall MD PhD was the visionary, who created and implemented freeworldu.org. He raised funds, and provided funds from his family Foundation to establish this one of a kind accelerated learning online program. His vision originated with journeys to third world countries to see what could be done to facilitate the education, health, and self sustaining governments each country needed to create their own free countries, yet maintain their ancient traditions and beliefs. His thought upon coming home was that just to create adequate health care there was not enough money in the world, education was going to have to come into play. He created an online study system of accelerated learning to help world medical students pass their examinations, and get support to become the much needed doctors all over the globe. People kept asking him to provide similar programs for nurses, teachers, leadership, and students of all ages. He designed freeworldu.org with other doctors, medical students, teachers, and community members active in community service in education, health and welfare. He designed and built his own server system, and worked with others to create a system that could easily be used on a cell pone which were just beginning to advance in capabilities. How much less expensive to sent ONE cell phone, with accompanying WI FI capability to a whole school, than to attempt to educate hundreds of people of all ages. The curriculum was based on the curriculum requirements for high school graduation in the State of California, each of the unit designers and support system mentors was a credentialed teacher.

The pay for use system used by many home school programs was phenomenally successful. Other programs utilized the system for children failing in the regular public and private school systems. Often used to help youth and children who were behind, probation and other programs working with high risk youth began to see unheard of growth and understanding, one year of online study putting their clients in grade level, or above ranking in their own school systems. The secret of this program is that it is NOT electronic flash cards. The system is designed to facilitate for the student to identify areas of lack, and to learn those areas, to build higher education upon.

Just as a house can not be built roof first, education can not be built without a solid foundation. Almost every subject requires a solid foundational base, and the computer programs are designed to identify for each question and unit what the success or lack is for each student. The computer system then directs them to the foundation units and facilitates their building in the stable foundation.

Even students with top grades in one area having a lack in one of the foundational areas will be stressed and suffer failures along their educational path unless they find and build the areas that are lacking in both knowledge, and accomplishment.

This system was marketed to several foundations and public education systems at very low cost, and free training for its use. Instead, systems of electronic flashcarding were created that fail to do what factoid unit education accomplishes. While rote repetition can create a student who can pass tests for a short period of time, the inner learning required to establish the solid foundation of knowledge and skill AT LEARNING is missing.

Our programs utilize our own special education and hands on science methods, as well as utilize freeworldu.org for all students to raise to their own goals and standards in their own schools.

ADDITIONAL uses of these programs:

Just as the Directors were needing medical care and put the program into hiatus, an amazing woman decided to quit her business career and start an equine therapy program. She visited Spirit Horse II, and has been an awesome inspiring help to both horses and heroes over the eight years that the program has been online and on telephone crisis work, this woman and her daughter founded and have networked into more than 350

Horse4heroes member stables. These programs give free, or low cost riding and treatment programs to veterans, first responders, high risk youth and educational programs and events to inspire others in community service and overcoming whatever negatives life has thrown at them.

There are several programs developed over the past twenty years using the written program of Spirit Horse to develop their own animal assisted programs.

Three of our major Board members, Chris Thomas, Real Estate Broker, Community volunteer, and the catalyst with Redevelopment to inspire the first 48 Acre site for veterans, Miriam Negri, Founding Directing Architect of IDESIGN, as well as Los Angeles Redevelopment Specialist on many projects including the Domestic Violence Survivors program, the new facades to Little Tokyo and the development of new sports areas across the city of Los Angeles, and Susan Thompson, retired Alabama State Human Resources Planner, Maria Trejo, initiator of the idea of Homes for Heroes, small single homes to be utilized for treatment and support of veterans by veterans are all thanked for their dedication and help towards our high risk youth, veterans, and first responders and their families in designing these programs. ALL of the volunteer psychiatrists, therapists, social workers and volunteers are thanked for their help in these projects.

Habitat for Humanity, and Rebuilding Together, Bank of the West, where our account representative and his Branch manager were both veterans, and all the veterinarians, and horse owners who helped with the programs are warmly remembered and thanked. The many veterans, with their own programs, and the many volunteer program leaders who worked with us to make every event, and the vision of the? 48 Acres" move forward.

BIO of our Director:

Patricia McLaughlin was injured and off work by the request of the school where one of the special education students had assaulted her, until her surgeries and injuries were completed. At that time she had been an active special education associate for the equine therapy program and mentoring, as well as education projects of Spirit Horse II.

Following the request by Congress to come and address a panel of Congresspersons on the needs and our thoughts on resolving the problems of veterans and their families, Patricia paid for several of the Homes for Heroes and Women Veteran California members to travel by air, stay in Washington DC hotels, and eat to facilitate their attendance at a panel she had to attend in a wheelchair following surgery for injuries from the assault. This money was never repaid as promised.

Many times Patricia was invited to attend, and comment at panels for local, state and Federal committees to learn what the problems were, and thoughts on how to resolve those problems and answer those needs. All of this travel was at her own expense.

One of the Congresspersons asked National Homes for Heroes/Spirit Horse II to step out of their comfort zone, working with other projects, and in a special disabled challenge Charter project initiated and implemented by Spirit Horse and then Spirit Horse II and get their own 501 3 c. IRS promised they would help, and at first did.

While filling out the paperwork required for the application, the Board met at the home of one of the members, and Patricia was in the restroom when the line that asked who was the director was reached. As in the military, those not fast enough to step back, get the volunteer jobs they did not intend to acquire. Patricia became the Director. Even while in surgery for spinal cord cancer, she answered her phone in the critical care unit and dealt with issues as required.

Until it became necessary for her to accept early retirement from her career job, due to the injuries of the assault, which turned out to be a blessing as the MRI showed the minute and growing spinal cord cancer at an early enough time to be treated successfully after one relapse, Patricia was still going to return to finish out her career as a special education teacher.

Patricia, at age three caught her left hand in a mangle. She was caught in the machine, and burned to a point that no one thought she would be able to keep her arm, let alone her hand. Doctors new to the restoration and salvation of burns, due to the new techniques being found for soldiers injured in battle, used these new and developing techniques. Patricia spent more than twenty years having surgery after surgery as each time her body and hand grew, the new grafts and repairs had to be created. Just following one of these surgeries, while on break from college to become a teacher, Patricia jumped on a bus, and went to SELMA as part of the white student support to stand up for the equal civil rights for all movement in America.

Patricia, upon graduation worked in special education programs, raising the hopes, and skills of both parents and children in schools until assigned the White Mountain Apache school where she was so beloved she was called "THE White Apache" by the people of that nation that could only be reached by narrow, scary roads along the lip of a volcano crater that led to the area the Native Nation had been doled out as theirs.

Working on respect for students and parents, Patricia has developed her own methods of anchoring young and old alike to their own traditions and beliefs, while learning the dominant economic culture and educational academic skills needed to become self sustaining in a world oppositional to their own.

After living in Japan for some period of time, and returning to educational work in Arizona, Patricia married a second generation Chinese American from San Franciso Chinatown. Her daughter Leung Fa is a career Marine biologist with a current job learning policy of environmental and marine biological policy in State government.

A lifetime Girl Scout Masterlleader, Patricia as facilitated for women and girls who have not had the opportunity of a Mother in scouting to participate and learn skills from the programs developed by Daisy, the Founder of both the Welsh Girl Guides and The Girl Scouts of America so girls and women would have a hope and opportunity in a world one of the original Welsh Girl Guides told us was based on Daisy meeting a young woman who pleaded for help, so she would not just end up in manual labor all her life, with no hope except manual labor, the sex trades and to die alone by the side of a road.

Sharing her disability, pain, and the prejudices against her openly with the high risk youth and veterans has helped them in many ways to be inspired to get up their own hope and build dreams, and accomplish them. Patricia is a true community hero. She carries one dollar bills and coupons to share with homeless when she sees them, and often shares care and hope as she greets them by name, and hands over a dollar and a coupon for a meal at a local restaurant.

Paul, one of the first veterans met in the program was a young vet, with cancer, who because he had been honest and told the worker filling out his application at the Veteran's Administration that he sat on a corner each day to beg the $10 a friend charged him to sleep on the floor until he got into his Veterans program was inspirational to Pat to get out and go to Congress panels and short as she is, shake the suit sleeve of Congresspersons, and tell them what is really going on after a meeting in which many groups gave glowing reports of what they were doing to serve the veterans. NONE of those programs had help for Paul. We thank Congressman Tanaka, Senator McCain, and Senator Sanders for their work in finally getting improved services for the veterans, and care for Paul.

This personal dedication is what Patricia is about. She currently has two ten year old boxers that both need surgery after their young veteran owner took his own life. He had asked his sister to watch the dogs, and brought them over a couple of days, no one heard from him again. She contacted his apartment manager, who with police found him, passed away by his own hand. The sister was not able to keep the dogs and asked a boxer rescue to help. They found a foster, but the foster home dog said NO, and fought with the boxers. Patricia was asked to take them for a few days, that was a few months ago, they ate her expensive custom blinds, her screens, and tore around the house, telling her dog, THIS is now OUR dog bed. So she figured it out. The dogs need surgery, and while the rescues raise the money and get that taken care of and a home together can be guaranteed for them. Patricia has kept them in sorrow, and memory of their loss, hopefully to give them happy years together their last couple of years. The veterinarian told her that Boxers live ten to twelve years, and these two are ten. The dogs are so eager to see young men, they are then saddened when it is not who they are expecting. This is true community service, especially for a senior, retired person just out of another surgery this past year.

# "happily ever after…"

can be as simple as feeding and caring for two old dogs who lost their young lifelong owner.

## PROGRAMS

Whether it is your own family, your extended family, the people on your block, or in your apartment complex, it is necessary to become involved and involve other to help all to "live happily ever after".

In our racial tension and gang abatement programs we left the norm of blaming, hating, and being outraged. We went to those who cause the negatives and asked them to help us build something more positive for themselves, for their families, neighbors, cities, states and our nation.

The initial study was done in the late 1980's. Prisoners in jails and prison programs were asked, "how could YOU have changed the direction of your life so you did not end up here?" and "how could society have facilitated for the changes needed to make sure you did not end up here?" Prisoners asked in the first group surveyed and interviewed loved the idea so much they volunteered to do the surveys and interviews themselves behind bars.

Other books by this author, and/or with this consulting group to help people learn to live

# "happily ever after..."

**Reassessing and Restructuring Public Agencies** is the result of several years of research by the author for what she calls a Puffoey Degree...The author was the first Native American California Rez woman to graduate from law school. Passing the first half of the Bar in 20 minutes, it is a 3 hour exam, the author then contracted Toxic Shock Syndrome and spent the next eight years learning to walk and talk well enough to hold hot horses for her younger son, who was becoming a horse trainer at the tracks and show barns in S. California.

The author learned to walk again by holding on to strollers and taking walks with single mothers of diverse backgrounds, and nationalities, as they walked around the city and parks, gathering bottles and cans to pay publishing costs on their own single Mother newsletter "Yo Mama".

Teaching young Mothers how to read to their children and how to do homework with their children, as well as how to get motivated and do the paperwork needed to make their own dreams come true, in career, and to buy their own homes as she learned to read and write, and type again..........

was considered by the Judge in her disability case for Social Security. The Judge found that not only was she permanently disabled, with a prognosis of impending death, but that due to the amount of volunteer work she had done, in her own initiated and implemented programs for Racial Tension and Gang Abatement as well as the Single Mother programs that she NEVER had to work again at less than a full administrator, or lawyer. No one, least of all the author expected that she would live with the brain and heart scarring from the high fevers and staph enzymes of the disease TSS.

This book was written as a book for citizenship classes for high risk youth, veterans, and new citizens from the material the author collected in her volunteer work, and the material researched for her Pafooey Degree, which she did not get, even with a 3.74 overall grade point average, even with every class removing points for grammar and APA when the school did NOT provide the promised ADA Brain injury support program or editors which were part of her agreement as she enrolled in their program.

This book is written at Fourth Grade level for students, parents, and high risk youth to learn about our country and our world, and what it means to be a good citizenship. There are some of the programs the Foundation and Development Center have initiated and worked on. Other books by this author: Carousel Horse, Rez Cheeze, Dollars in the Streets (edit for Lydia Caceres, the first woman horse trainer for racing thoroughbreds). Carousel Two, about Veterans in equine therapy, and Still Spinning, about Women Veterans are expected to be published in the spring of 2019.

**OTHER BOOKS BY AUTHOR**

***Reassessing and Restructuring Public Agencies***: What to do to save our Country

***Carousel Horse***: a teaching inclusive book about equine therapy

***Spirit Horse II***: Equine therapy manuals and workbooks

***Could This Be Magic***: a VERY short book about the time I spent with VAN HALEN

***Dollars in the Streets-Lydia Caceres*** Edited by Author about first woman horse trainer at Belmont Park

***Addicted to Dick***: a healing book quasi Twelve Step for women with addiction to mean men

***Addicted to Dick-2018 Edition*** Self help and training manual for women who allow men to torture, molest and kill their children

**BOOKS TO BE RELEASED:**

*America CAN live happily ever after*: first in series of Americans resolving all the issues

*America CAN live happily ever after 2*: Second in series of HOW to go out and BE equal, and to part of the OF the, BY the and FOR the People our Constitution guarantees us. If the school is not teaching your children, go down and read, do math, join a science project, do lunchtime Scouting for the kids, go sit in the hallways with your smart phone and take lovely action video for the parents of kids who do not behave. More. Many suggestions from parents, and how to fundraise.

*Carousel Two*: Equine therapy for veterans

*Still Spinning*: Equine therapy for women veterans

*Legal Ethics*: An Oxymoron???

*Friend Bird*: A children's book about loneliness and how to conquer it (adults will love it too)

*Kids* Anonymous and Kids Jr. quasi twelve step books for and by youth and teens

12 Steps Back from Betrayal from Brothers at Arms and 12 Steps Home two quasi twelve step books and work books created by author and veterans, and author's Father for Native American and other veterans

**BIG LIZ**: The Leader of the Gang  Racial Tension and Gang Abatement work by author

PLEASE join the tee shirt contests by checking the web sites on the books and contacting the link provided.  WE love children, teens and adults helping us to give our classes free, and spread the word of our work.  ALL of our work is done through education projects by our high risk youth, veterans and first responders page NATIONAL HOMES FOR HEROES/SPIRIT HORSE II.  We are just getting back to full work due to cancer of the two Directors and vehicle accidents and our stable burning down in a forest fire a couple of years ago.  We promise to get more organized as we move along. 2019is our first year of taking nominations and awarding a Keiry Equine Therapy Award.  We will also need poster and tee shirt designs for that.  See Carousel Horse and Spirit Horse II links to nominate a program.  God bless us, as Tiny Tim said, Everyone.

Printed in the United States
By Bookmasters